Home Helps

HOME
SECURITY

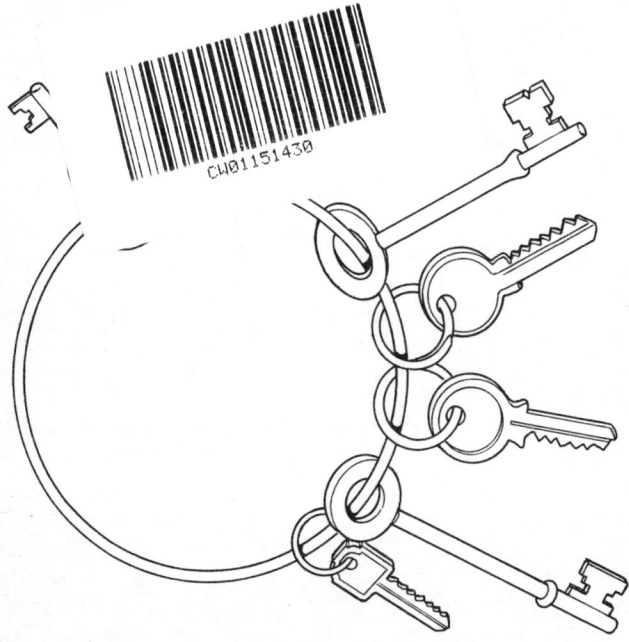

Ward Lock Limited · London

© Text & illustrations Ward Lock Ltd 1988

First published in Great Britain in 1988
by Ward Lock Limited, 8 Clifford Street
London W1X 1RB, an Egmont Company

All Rights Reserved. No part of this publication
may be reproduced, stored in a retrieval system,
or transmitted, in any form or by any means,
electronic, mechanical, photocopying, recording,
or otherwise, without the prior permission of the
Copyright owners.

Designed by Anita Ruddell

Illustrated by Peter Bull Art

Text filmset in Baskerville No. 2
by MS Filmsetting Limited, Frome, Somerset
Printed and bound in Great Britain by
Richard Clay, Bungay, Suffolk

British Library Cataloguing in Publication Data
Charlish, Anne
  Home security.
  1. Home accidents. Great Britain.
  Prevention   2. Dwellings, Great Britain.
  Security measures.
  I. Title   II. Series
  643'.028'9

  ISBN 0-7063-6674-3

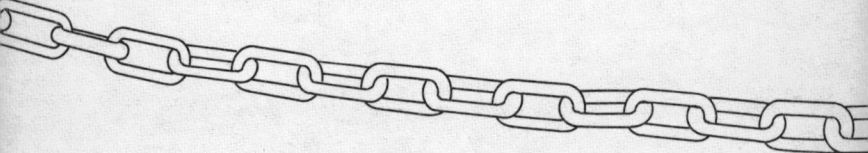

CONTENTS

Introduction *4*
1 Security Counsel *5*
2 Playing Safe *8*
3 Fire Control *17*
4 Away on Holiday *29*
5 Doorstops *33*
6 Window Dressing *40*
7 Illegal Entry *47*
8 Alarm Bells *54*
9 External Forces *71*
10 How did they get in? *82*

Appendix: Useful organizations and addresses *90*
Index *95*

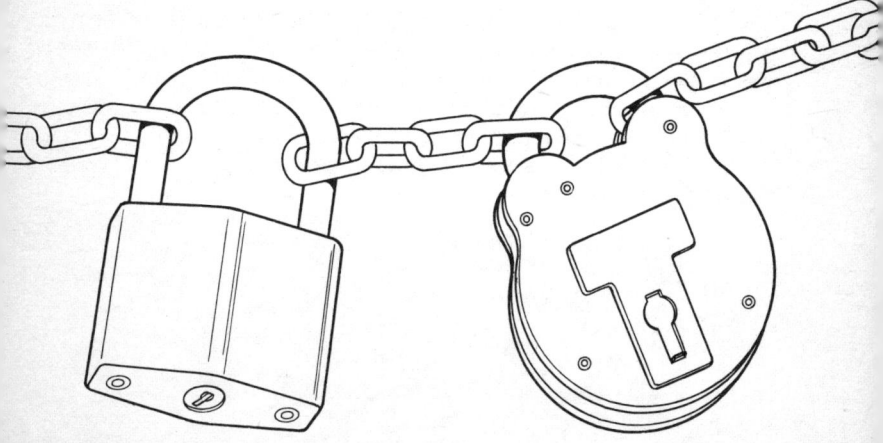

INTRODUCTION

We all regard our homes as places in which to relax and to enjoy our friends and families – essentially, private places. But what happens if our homes are violated by an intruder?

Burglarly is now so common that 500,000 homes are broken into in Britain every year and the police admit that there is little they can do either to prevent it happening to you or to recover your valued possessions.

So, this is the time to act: all of us can improve the security of our homes at no expense at all by simply being careful. Avoid leaving tell-tale signs for the opportunist thief indicating that you are not at home – such as the milk left upon the step in the morning, an empty garage with the door left open, or the hall light left on at night while the rest of the house is in darkness. This book alerts you to what burglars look for and how to combat the ever-increasing menace of such an intrusion into your home.

Home Security also describes how you can improve the security of your home in a variety of ways in return for a modest investment. Don't wait, as so many people do, until after you have been burgled to take the matter of home security as seriously as you do the happiness and security of your family.

A chapter is devoted to preventing fire in the home as an essential aspect of home security. The majority of domestic fires are preventable and yet several hundred people die each year as a result of a fire in the home. Again, simple common sense precautions can do much to make sure that this never happens to you.

All of us should be safe and happy in our own homes: with good home security we are.

· 1 ·

SECURITY COUNSEL

You have locked yourself out of the house by mistake, it's late at night or pouring with rain, and you decide that you will have to break in: how do you do it?

1 manoeuvre the slightly open kitchen window?

2 slip a plastic credit card past the latch?

3 get a ladder from the garage and climb up to an open bedroom window?

4 go round the back of the house and force the back door?

5 put your hand through the letterbox and open the latch?

6 get a small child to slip through a tiny open window – it need only measure 15 or 18 cm (6 or 7 in) deep?

7 climb up on to a low flat roof and get through a window?

Congratulations! You managed to get in without having to call a locksmith or the police and without even having to break a window. But if *you* can do it, think how easy and quick it would be for a professional burglar to get in.

Even if the professional burglar does not use any of the seven routes listed above, he (and most burglars are men) will not feel too bad about breaking a window or forcing the front door.

A burglary these days is such a commonplace event – 52 taking place every hour of the day – that the police just do not have the resources to follow up most leads. It is therefore unlikely that you will ever see any stolen property again. Half a million British households are burgled every year, and that figure is really not so surprising when you consider burglary is a comparatively quick and easy crime, particularly for the opportunist, with what are often rich rewards of jewelry, furs and hi-fi to be sold on.

It is often said, rather apathetically, that if a burglar wants to get in, he will – and this is theoretically true. Where this belief falls down in practice, however, is that the majority of burglaries are not planned jobs but the result of someone spotting the opportunity for quick gain and seizing it. So, the crucial issue is to make your house or flat as secure as possible, without turning it into a fortress, in order to *deter* or *delay* burglars. Burglars are mostly lazy by nature and they will not persevere with a thoroughly locked house with a burglar alarm when they can see a more inviting prospect a few doors down that has a window ajar and no alarm.

Although burglary with violence occurs, the majority of burglaries take place when the householder is likely to be out, between 10 am and 4 pm. No burglar wants to be confronted and when he is, he tends to run away. Making your house as secure as possible to protect it while you are out, therefore, is recommended as a means of playing for time: in other words, it is true that the determined burglar would gain entry in any case, but your objective should be to make his task as difficult and as time-consuming as possible in the hope that you will return and frighten him off before he has had a chance to stuff your jewelry into his pockets.

There are a number of levels at which you can make your home secure, most of which enhance the others. The first basic level is that of not making it obvious that you are either out or on holiday by having curtains closed through the day, for example, or the hall light on while the rest of the house is in darkness. Level 1 protection, which should be regarded as part of your lifestyle, is described in the next chapter. Level 2 protection requires you to be just a little more ingenious and to some extent to rely on the help of neighbours in making your house appear occupied when it is not, especially when you are away on a fortnight's holiday (*see Chapter 4*).

Whether your home has the appearance of being occupied or not, it will still need Level 3 protection in the form of physical deterrents to illegal entry. These physical deterrents can take the form of locks, chains, hinge bolts and so on for doors; locks, grilles or bars for windows; and protection for other vulnerable areas such as skylights and roofs. All these aspects of physical protection are described in Chapters 5, 6 and 7.

Much depends upon what sort of area you live in when you are deciding how far you should go with security for the home. Good physical deterrents and a common sense approach to lifestyle may be enough to save you from the upset of a burglary in a fairly rural area. If you live in a city, however, you would be well advised to go beyond Level 3 to Level 4, which means installing a burglar alarm. The only truly effective burglar alarm is the one that is backed up with good physical deterrents, and which also rings at a central station, to alert

Security Counsel

the police without actually ringing in the house. In this way, police should be able to catch the intruders. A burglar alarm that simply rings loudly, however, is often sufficiently off-putting to a burglar, and he will prefer to go to the house that does not have an alarm. The pros and cons of alarm systems and their variations are described in Chapter 8.

There are other aspects of home security beyond these four levels, however, and these are dealt with in Chapters 3 and 9. Essentially, it is wise to protect not just your house but any surrounding garden as well. If, for example, you succeed in scaring off a potential intruder before he even gets as far as the front door, and perhaps damaging it in the process of trying to get in, the money you have spent on outside protection can be regarded as well spent. Apart from outside security, you should also consider the question of securing your garage from thieves and, especially important these days, securing your car both for itself and for any car radio or car stereo. The theft of car radios is now so common that it is surprising car manufacturers still do not fit a good car alarm as well as locks.

The last, and perhaps the most important of all aspects of home security, is guarding your house and family against the possibility of fire. Many, many cases of house fires could have been prevented if straightforward protective measures had been taken. It is very much cheaper and easier to install a smoke alarm, to signify the start of a fire, than to install a burglar alarm (or even to have a really good quality lock on the front door) and it should be regarded as a priority for every household (*see* Chapter 3). There is never anything to be gained by taking risks either with fire prevention or burglary deterrence: playing safe should always be the principle.

·2·

PLAYING SAFE

Your attitude to security if you have never been burgled will be in stark comparison to someone who has suffered in this way. The person who has already been burgled will know that it is not simply a matter of losing items that can be replaced by insurance, changing locks, mending windows, dealing with the police and clearing up the mess, but the feeling that a most personal area of one's life, the home, has been violated by strangers.

If you have never been burgled and do not yet appreciate the importance of securing your home from this sort of intrusion, your attitude to security may be summed up in the statements, 'If they want to get in, they will anyway' and 'I've got nothing worth stealing'.

NOTHING WORTH STEALING?

How many of us can honestly run down this list and say that we do not possess any of the items?

- jewelry
- furs
- silver
- antique clocks
- passport
- television
- stereo
- video
- portable radio
- portable tape recorder
- camera
- calculator
- computer
- microwave

- chequebook and chequecard
- Eurocheques and Eurochequecard
- pedal bikes
- other outdoor equipment, including chainsaws, hedgetrimmers, ride-on mowers

If the demand is there, then there's a market and a burglar knows exactly how to fill it. Microwaves are increasingly popular targets and recently one man, not far out of London, was robbed of two ride-on mowers.

Most people do have something worth stealing and clearly a burglar is unlikely to break into a house in which it is obvious that there is really nothing. He only has to spot a stereo/video/TV through the sitting room window to decide that it is worth the effort.

Unfortunately, even if you really possessed absolutely nothing that was worth stealing, but the burglar had nevertheless decided that your home looked like a promising target, you would still have to deal with the broken door locks, windows and any mess. Burglars that are thwarted in this way have also been known to vent their spleen by stubbing out a cigarette on the carpet or urinating upon it, or by turning the house upside down and throwing things about.

A depressing thought indeed – but of course it may never happen to you. Home security, by definition, should mean securing your home against the possibility of burglary: it should be a preventative measure, rather than a remedy. It is a well-known fact, however, that the majority of people who have alarms installed and turn a keen eye to security do so because they have been recently burgled.

NOT AT HOME

All these things advertise that you are out:

- milk left upon the doorstep
- parcel left on the doorstep
- post or leaflets pushed halfway through the letterbox
- curtains closed during the daytime
- hall light left on at night while the rest of the house is left in darkness (no one does that when they are in)
- empty dustbins with the lids left off by careless dustmen
- empty garage with the doors left open
- an Ansaphone with the message 'I'm out at the moment but ...'
- a notice on the front door 'Back in half an hour ...'

Not at Home

Tell-tale signs such as these indicate to a casual passer-by that the occupant is away.

- outside telephone bell that rings and rings (switch it off each time you go out or fit an Ansaphone)
- a dog confined to a pen or kennel (it is more likely to be running around freely if the owner is home)

All these things provide the burglar with the handy hint that he is looking for: the owner is out and so, if he's quick, he will probably get away with a few of your possessions. It is worth knowing that some 85 per cent of all burglaries are on-the-spot crimes, committed by an opportunist who has seized his chance. This type of burglar is the one who is quick to spot such indications of an empty house.

However, if you are the victim of a professionally planned burglary, avoiding such tell-tale signs becomes of less importance: the burglar and his accomplices will have cased the joint and monitored your movements. They will have already observed that you often go down to the shops at 10 in the morning or that the house is completely unattended from 8.30 am right through until the evening. If you have sufficient valuables for a burglar to consider a professional targeting, you should already have invested in each of the 4 levels of protection (*see* previous chapter).

COVERING YOUR TRACKS

All the little signs that indicate you are out can be eliminated with a little care. Arrange with the milkman to leave your milk somewhere out of sight from the casual passer-by; or if this is not possible and you live in a high-risk city area, consider buying the milk yourself with the rest of the groceries.

Ask delivery people to call when you are in or arrange that they deliver to a neighbour. You can ask the postman to make sure that the post is put right through the letterbox, but leafleting is impossible to control. All you can do is ask a neighbour who is around more often than you to push anything like that through.

Avoid presenting the house in such a way that it is obvious you are not there: so the curtains should be open during the day and closed at night and, during the evening, at least one or two lights should be on. Leave a battery-operated radio switched on.

If you have an Ansaphone, the message should be 'I'm in a meeting at the moment but ...'.

POSITIVE STEPS

Once you have looked critically at your everyday habits and tried to eradicate any signposts pointing to your absence, there are a number of other things you can do to protect your property before you decide which combination of Levels 1, 2, 3 and 4 you select. These include marking any possessions of great worth or sentimental value; making an inventory of jewelry, small antiques and other valuables; discussing community security with friendly neighbours and joining any local Neighbourhood Watch scheme; and asking the local Crime Prevention Officer (to be found at your police station) for a home visit to advise on security.

MAKING ONE'S MARK

Many of the things that you value can be marked in different ways, no matter whether they are large or small. The effectiveness of invisible marking agents was highlighted in one case not long ago when a policeman who had turned burglar was incriminated by an agent which had been applied to his clothing by other officers.

You can mark your personal possessions either by etching, die-stamping, branding, engraving, identification paint or by security marker pen. The security marker pen, which some Crime Prevention

Making One's Mark

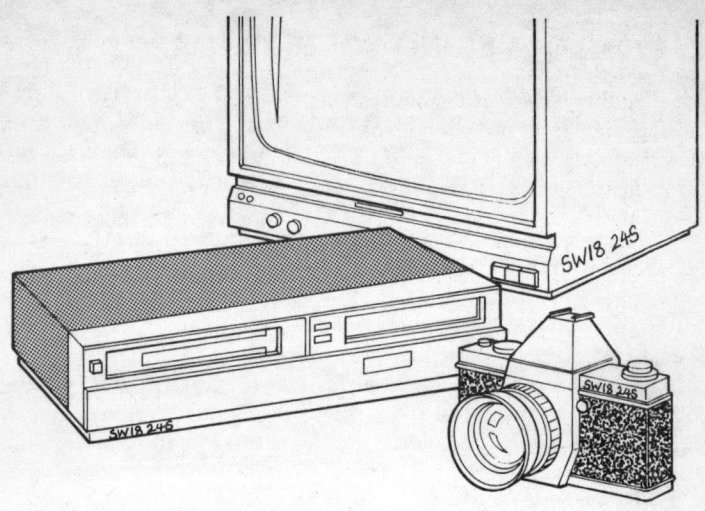

Mark valuable electrical goods and cameras with your postcode using an engraver or security marker.

Officers are able to lend to individuals for a 24 hour period, uses invisible ink and can only be read under an ultraviolet lamp.

Most materials, including glass, plastic, china, porcelain and enamel, as well as jewelry and any large items such as bicycles and mowers, can be marked by one of the processes mentioned above.

Diamond-tipped hand engravers can be bought from hardware stores and can be used to mark car windows, stereo systems, tape and cassette recorders, video, television, home computer and any other plastic or glass items, including precious glass such as decanters and bowls.

You may have some items which you are not sure how best to mark and in this case it is best to seek the advice of your Crime Prevention Officer. For very small items, which includes jewelry in particular, it may not be practicable and may be damaging to mark and the best thing in such cases is to take good clear photographs of the items. In the event of loss, you will have an easy means of providing the police with a description and, in addition, proof for a subsequent insurance claim that the item existed.

It would be a worthwhile precaution to photograph any unique and special item – such as porcelain, jewelry, gold and silver objects and pictures. It would also be wise to keep a record in a safe place of these special objects and of electronic equipment, giving a description, date purchased, from whom, sum paid and any further useful information, such as hallmarks for gold and silver jewelry and serial numbers for electrical and electronic equipment.

Rather than marking your name, which would prove a useful means of identification of the object only if it surfaced in the area of your local police station, you should mark items with your postcode followed by the number of your house or the first two letters of its name. For example, if your address was 8 Clifford Street, London W1X 1RB, you would mark W1X 1RB 8; if it was Bel Vista, Clifford Street, London W1X 1RB, you would mark W1X 1RB BE.

Once you have done this, you can obtain 'Marked Property' stickers from your local police station and these are best affixed near the main locks of front, side and back doors and any vulnerable windows, such as basements, for example.

NEIGHBOURHOOD WATCH

Your local Crime Prevention Officer will also be able to give you details of any local Neighbourhood Watch scheme and the name of the representative for your part of the street. He or she will also be able to alert you to particular hazards of the area, such as a nearby pub, for example, giving rise to spates of car vandalism after closing time.

Each of us can help to fight crime, regardless of whether there is a local Neighbourhood Watch scheme, by simply being observant. If you see someone putting their shoulder to a front door, and you don't recognize that person as the owner, dial 999 immediately, ask for the police and give the address as clearly as possible. If you should hear the sound of breaking glass coming from a nearby house, it is reasonable to assume that a burglary is taking place. If you see someone moving a number of large objects out of a house, such as televisions, other electrical equipment, or even pictures, for example, you should consider the possibility that the house is being burgled and dial 999. If what looks like a removal van arrives at your neighbour's house, and she has not mentioned anything about selling the house or moving, you should be immediately suspicious and either contact your neighbour as swiftly as possible or call the police.

If you make it clear that you intend to fight crime in these different ways, you can reasonably hope that your neighbours will be influenced and reciprocate in the same way if your own house appears to be threatened. Word may get around in the local criminal fraternity, too, that people have eyes like hawks in your particular area.

MAKING A NOISE

One way of giving your house or flat the appearance of being occupied is through noise and an easy, safe way of doing this is to leave a battery-operated radio playing in one of the downstairs rooms. It may well prove enough to deter the opportunist burglar.

Another way, if you have a dog, is to let him either roam around freely in the house or at least unchained in the kitchen. Burglars are *said* to be wary of any dog, regardless of whether it is an Alsatian or a cocker spaniel – although having said that many burglaries have in fact been committed in the presence of a dog.

NEITHER IN NOR OUT

Burglaries commonly take place on sunny summer afternoons when you may not actually be in the house but somewhere around it. The opportunist burglar need only hear the sound of a lawnmower, or observe a relaxed outdoor lunch taking place, to take the calculated risk of simply walking in, helping himself, and getting away.

So, always make sure that the front door is securely locked. If your garden is so large that you cannot always keep French windows or the back door in sight, at least close them and leave a radio playing in one of the downstairs rooms. A burglar can be in and out with a sizeable haul in under a quarter of an hour, so never relax in the thought, 'I won't be long'.

FROM UNDER YOUR VERY EYES

Well, almost. It is becoming increasingly common for burglars to raid a house while it is occupied. This is partly in response to houses often being better secured than they used to be – that is, while the inhabitants are out. When they return home, however, they do not realize that the back door that has been left open for the cat or the dog is just as convenient for the burglar. If you are having dinner, the noise that can make and the length of time it takes to eat, provides the perfect backdrop for the burglar to pop quietly upstairs. Equally, you may be sitting engrossed in a TV programme, or listening to loud music (perhaps using headphones), when an intruder arrives. He will often make for the master bedroom first because jewelry, conveniently small and portable, is so often kept upon the dressing table.

This type of theft is now a common occurrence and should not be dismissed lightly.

FIRE

Guarding your home against the possibility of fire is an essential aspect of home security. A fire in your house is potentially very much more dangerous and destructive than a burglary and every effort should be made to prevent it.

Many houses these days have modern sitting room furniture upholstered with polyurethane foam. Once smouldering, this type of foam releases a highly poisonous gas, called hydrogen cyanide, which is *immediately* fatal if there is as much as 0·027 per cent in the air, and fatal within ten minutes if the concentration is 0.018. Common causes of fire include inflammable upholstered furniture being ignited by a spark from a fire, match or cigarette or by a faulty electrical appliance igniting furniture.

Fires have been caused by children setting fire to paper, bedclothing, their own clothes, books or the contents of cupboards. They are also commonly caused by a cigarette not properly extinguished, smoking in bed, paraffin heaters, faulty electrical appliances such as electric blankets or toasters and faulty electrical wiring. Once electrical wiring is faulty, with sparks appearing or a fizzing sound emanating from sockets, the insulation is evidently ineffective and a fire is a likely consequence. Such fires can ignite carpets and other soft furnishings so that the spread can be very rapid.

Playing safe is a rule that must never be broken in the context of safeguarding your home from fire and this is discussed fully in the next chapter. Basic wise precautions include:

1 Don't smoke unless there is an ashtray close at hand. Make sure that the cigarette or cigar is thoroughly extinguished before you leave the room.

2 Never smoke in bed.

3 Don't have hazardous heating devices, such as paraffin heaters, if there are children in the house.

4 Never allow children access to matches or any other form of possible ignition, such as cigarette lighters.

5 Make sure that all fires are thoroughly extinguished before you go to bed, and close all internal doors (which would prevent the spread of a fire as fire needs oxygen).

6 Don't use any faulty electrical appliances. Unplug them at the socket and either get them fixed or throw them away.

7 Have your electrical wiring checked if you do not know when the flat or house was last rewired. Wiring cannot be expected to last for more than about twenty years.

Fire

8 Have electric blankets serviced every second summer. Faults develop easily with wear.

9 Never sleep on top of an electric overblanket and never have an electric underblanket on top of you. You should follow the manufacturer's instructions rigorously and always make sure that it is switched off, unless it is of the type that the manufacturer states can be kept on during the night.

10 Never heat a pan of boiling fat to smoking point, when cooking chips for example: this is already at danger point. The fat should be hot, not smoking.

11 Always keep a fire blanket in the kitchen just in case of a fire on the hob. Do not try to immerse the pan in water once it is alight as this could make matters worse.

12 Invest in a smoke alarm – for less than the cost of dinner out for two. (Smoke alarms are described in Chapter 3: Fire Control.)

13 It is wise to keep a fire extinguisher in the kitchen and to be familiar with how it works.

14 All chimneys should be swept regularly to prevent the possibility of a chimney fire.

15 If you are caught upstairs in a burning house, you *must* jump from the window without delay. If smoke or flames can be seen from the stairs, make no attempt to negotiate the stairs. You could be overcome by smoke or poisonous fumes within seconds and asphyxiated. Never go back to pick up anything. If there are any children around, they may well be unwilling to go downstairs, even if you judge it safe to do so, or to jump from an upstairs window: in such a case, pick them up or move them by force.

16 Lastly, when you plan the physical deterrents to burglary, be sure to think of the implications in the event of fire. Fitting non-removable bars to basement windows, or to any others (with the possible exception of a child's bedroom), cannot be recommended as this would mean being trapped in the building in the event of a fire.

·3·

FIRE CONTROL

Many people would argue that although the risk of a serious fire in the home is fairly small when compared with, say, a burglary, the very real danger associated with all fires should make effective fire prevention and control a top priority for us all.

Some simple precautions that you can take in order to prevent the outbreak of fire are outlined in Chapter 2, but this chapter describes the prevention of fire in the home, fire hazards, fire fighting and fire escape routes in more depth and detail.

SMOKE DETECTORS

No home should be without a smoke detector, which is a device that sounds a loud and insistent bleep as soon as smoke activates it. (There are also heat detectors on the market, but a smoke detector is the better investment as it is likely to be triggered earlier than a heat detector in an outbreak of fire.)

There are two types of smoke detector for the home: ionization smoke detectors and optical smoke detectors. It has been shown that ionization smoke detectors react slightly more quickly to a hot blaze – such as would occur if a chip pan full of boiling fat caught fire – while optical detectors appear to be quicker to detect a smouldering fire, such as would occur if a lighted cigarette fell down the back or side of upholstered furniture and smouldered prior to the piece of furniture bursting into flame.

It is possible to buy detectors that combine both methods and these are ideal for fire detection. Dual detectors are best electrically connected to each other, so that only one of them needs to be triggered to activate the alarm.

Smoke detectors depend on the method of power used for their reliability. Some inexpensive units are powered by batteries; some units are run from the mains electricity supply; and others are powered

Smoke Detectors

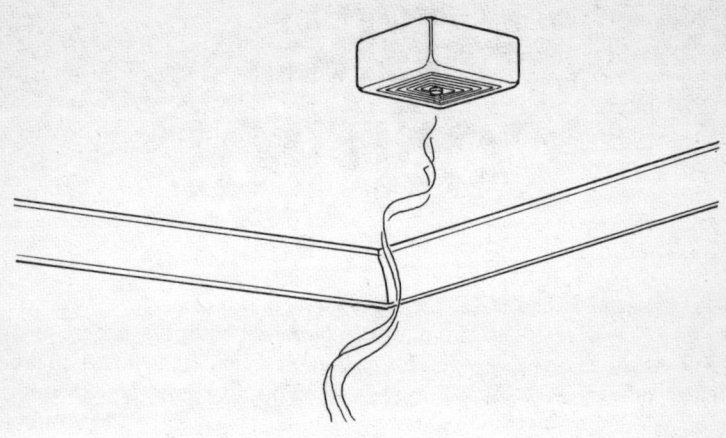

Simple smoke detector devices are now readily available from hardware stores.

by the mains, but contain a standby battery so that if the mains fail, which is possible in a fire, the battery powers the unit. Clearly, the third is the most reliable method; the second is acceptable provided that your house has been rewired in the last fifteen years, that you have no faulty wiring and that you are not subject to regular power cuts. The first type of unit works only as well as the batteries – you must check them as a matter of routine and it should incorporate a device to sound the bleep alarm when the batteries are running down. You should test a battery powered alarm each time you return from a weekend or a few days away, in case you have missed the low battery signal.

Whichever unit you decide to buy, it should conform to BS 5446 and installation should ideally conform to BS 5839 Part 1.

If you decide that the investment is worth it, perhaps if you have a very large house, children or elderly people in the household or if you are away regularly, you may have a mains powered system connected direct to the fire emergency service by automatic link-up. This works similarly to an automatic burglar alarm link-up with the police; and there is less likelihood of false alarms than with a burglar alarm.

False alarms can be triggered by someone blowing cigarette smoke directly into the detector; the amount of smoke generated by a number of people, say, at a party; when the detector has been wrongly positioned – in a boiler house, in any room subject to steam, such as a

Smoke Detectors

kitchen or bathroom, above heaters, radiators or airconditioning vents; by a toaster burning the toast.

The location of your smoke detector is crucial. Firstly, if your house is quite large, you may well need more than one. The next principle is that you must be able to hear the alarm from all the bedrooms in your home. Test that you will be able to hear it, even if you are asleep, by having someone hold it in position and then listen from each bedroom, lying down on the bed, with a radio on. You should be able to hear its insistent bleep over the sound of the radio; if you cannot, it is unlikely to wake you.

If you are fitting one detector, you should choose a spot between the likely sources of fire, which are the kitchen and living rooms, and the bedrooms. It should be no more than ten paces (7 m/23 ft) from the door to any room in which a fire could start. The reason for this is that the detector must be able to activate its alarm quickly so that your escape route, usually the stairs if it is at night, is not cut off by smoke before you have had a chance to leave the house.

If you are fitting one detector in a two-storey house, it is usually best sited in the hallway above the bottom of the staircase. Test it to make sure that it can be heard in all the bedrooms above the sound of a radio. If you cannot hear it, you should link in a second detector on the upstairs floor to the downstairs detector. This is worthwhile in any case as a downstairs detector is unlikely to detect the outbreak of fire in a upstairs bedroom – such as could be caused by a faulty electric blanket or lighted cigarette. Remember that even if you do not smoke, guests may do so; and they are just as likely to smoke in their bedroom as downstairs.

Because smoke detectors can be falsely triggered by steam and heat if they are sited in a kitchen, you should not fit one in that room: however, it's also the most likely place for a fire, so, when you are deciding where to position your detector/s, make sure that there is one within ten paces of the kitchen.

If you are undecided about where to fix your smoke detectors, consult the Fire Prevention Officer with your local fire brigade. The fire services have a preventative role as well as a fire fighting responsibility. If you prefer to have your detectors professionally supplied and fitted for you, approach a security company, such as Chubb, many of whom fit both burglar and fire alarms, or a specialist fire alarm company. You can obtain the details of local companies from your local fire brigade or from the Yellow Pages under the heading of Fire Alarms. Always obtain at least three estimates and compare the specifications recommended by each company.

DO'S AND DON'TS

1 The detector should be fixed on the ceiling at least 30 cm (12 in) from any wall or ceiling light fitting. If it is designed for wall mounting, it should be between 15–30 cm (6–12 in) below the ceiling.

2 Put the detector, ideally, where you can reach it safely for testing. Locating it above a stairwell is not ideal.

3 Do not position the detector in any room that is subject to extremes of temperature or condensation as this can trigger false alarms, eg boiler house, unheated cloakroom, bathroom, shower room, kitchen, garage; and not above heaters or radiators.

4 *Do* seek professional advice if you are not sure where it should be.

FIRE HAZARDS

Fire in the home can nearly always be avoided, and yet, sadly, there are more than 50,000 accidental fires in British homes, which kill some 650 people and injure well over 6,000. Some people manage to escape physical injury only to sustain lasting emotional trauma. Of all deaths by fire in Britain, nearly 80 per cent occur in the home. Of all the causes investigated, it has been shown that building design is responsible for very few; fires are caused largely by the contents and the lifestyle of the occupants of the home.

DOING THE HOUSEWORK

1 Do not put any newspapers, clothes, flammable liquids or spray cans near heaters or open fires.

2 Make sure that curtains and other furnishings are well away from all types of heater and open fires.

3 See that clutter is removed and the stairs and hallways kept free of obstructions at all times. Do not pile things on the stairs.

4 Do not store things like newspapers, rags and cleaning fluids beneath the stairs; if they were to catch fire, your escape route down the stairs would be blocked.

5 When you put out clothes to dry, keep them well away from heaters and open fires.

6 Do not use petrol or lighter fluid to dryclean clothes. Use a purpose-made non-inflammable cleaning fluid.

7 If you leave the room during ironing, turn off the iron and unplug it. Don't leave the flex stretched across the floor for someone to trip over.

Doing the Housework

The dangers of housework: a burning cigarette, an open fire or an iron could set this room ablaze.

8 Do not put the iron away hot, unless you store it in a purpose-made metal container attached to the wall.

9 Never connect an iron into a light fitting. Make sure that the flex is in good condition – if it is frayed, have it replaced before you next use it.

10 Aerosols and spray cans usually contain flammable liquids; do not, therefore, aim them at or near a naked flame, an open fire, a cigarette or any other source of heat. Never leave them near heaters, open fires or in direct sunlight. Never burn them or place them in an incinerator.

11 Never use an electrical appliance connected to a light fitting and never use an appliance if the cable or flex is damaged or frayed in any way. Replace the faulty cable or flex before you use the appliance.

12 If a hissing sound, or sparks, issue from a socket, turn off the appliance immediately and then turn off the socket switch before removing the plug. Have both the appliance and the socket itself inspected before you use either again. A faulty appliance can damage a socket which can in turn damage the next appliance used in it.

13 If you are a smoker, don't smoke when you are doing the housework. Your attention may be distracted and you may forget that you have put a cigarette down somewhere unusual. Never balance a cigarette on the edge of a desk or table.

JOBS AROUND THE HOUSE

Repairs and DIY are notorious for causing accidents, including fires in the home. Many of the recommendations made in the previous section apply to carrying out special projects around the house. However, in addition:

1 Do not join different pieces of flex together. Use a purpose-made flex connector, readily available from electrical shops and hardware stores.

2 Always fit fuses of the correct amps in plugs. As a rough guide, table lamps, blenders and mixers, stereo systems and sewing machines require 3 amp fuses, whilst 13 amp fuses are needed in irons, kettles, toasters, fridges, televisions and hoovers.

3 Keep your work area clean, tidy and clear of sawdust, shavings, oily rags, rags soaked in any flammable liquid and the liquids themselves. Keep such liquids – paint stripper, turps, meths, wood treatments, petrol, paraffin, kerosene, oil – in their original containers and make sure that the label is clearly visible. Those that do not come in a container should be kept in neatly labelled containers with tightly fitting lids.

4 Never smoke in a workshop or garage.

5 Never leave a blowlamp unattended.

6 Fit residual current devices (RCDs) to power tools and electric lawnmowers.

WATCHING THE CHILDREN

1 Keeping an eye on small children at all times is the single most important rule in preventing them accidentally starting a fire. It is nearly always *unattended* children who start fires.

2 Never let children use matches and lighters.

3 Fit dummy socket covers to the sockets if there are small children around in order to prevent them jamming something into the socket and starting an electrical fire.

4 Do not let children experiment with cooking unless you are in the kitchen with them.

5 Make sure that children understand the hazards of heaters and open fires. Do not use paraffin heaters if there are children around. Always have a fireguard around an open fire.

6 In a child's room, it is best to fit either a central heating radiator or a fixed wall heater high up on the wall well out of reach of the child, even if s/he climbs up onto a piece of furniture.

THE LIVING ROOM

The commonest cause of fires in living rooms is flammable furniture catching fire as a result of contact with a lighted cigarette or spark from an open fire.

1 It is vital to make sure that you extinguish cigarettes in an ashtray. Before you go to bed, check once again that all cigarettes are properly extinguished in the ashtray. Empty the ashtray the following morning, and avoid putting butts in a bin last thing at night.

2 Always have a fireguard in position around an open fire, whether there are children around or not.

3 Make sure that the fire is completely out before you go to bed.

4 Have soft furnishings, particularly curtains and foam-filled upholstered furniture, placed well away from open fires.

5 Remember that alcohol is a flammable liquid.

6 Candles are another hazard, although they look attractive. Make sure that they are well secured in their holders and nowhere near dried or cut flowers or soft furnishings.

7 Never put anything on top of electrical cable or flex: this includes furniture and carpets. If cable is covered in this way, it can become overheated and cause an electrical fire.

8 Consider carefully what you put on a mantelpiece over a fire. Toys may encourage children to stretch up for them – and their clothes, especially nightclothes, could catch alight. Mirrors and photographs will encourage adults to do the same thing. A large picture would be a safer bet; not a small one, however, as people might still go too close to the fire in order to look at it properly.

COOKING

Fires in the kitchen are commonly started by boiling fat catching fire.

1 Never fill a pan so full of fat that once it is boiling, there is a likelihood that the fat will splash on to a burner and become ignited.

2 Never leave a frying pan or chip pan of fat boiling if you leave the kitchen for a moment or two. Remove the pans from the heat first.

3 Keep the toaster clean and clear of crumbs so that there is not a residue of dry crumbs in the bottom which could start a fire the next time it is used.

4 Never let a child use the hob, oven or toaster if you are out of the room. Keep a discreet eye on them, and teach them good practice in the kitchen. For example, pan handles should not stick out at the front of the hob: turn them to one side.

GAS

If you smell gas, check that neither oven or hob has been left on accidentally; check, too, any gas fires, gas-powered water heaters and boilers in case a pilot light has gone out. If you cannot find the cause of the smell straightaway, turn off the supply at the meter and call the Gas Board, using the emergency number if it is outside their working hours. Do this even if it is at night.

The next step is to make sure that everyone has extinguished cigarettes and that there are no candles alight. Then open doors and windows to provide ventilation. Keep them open until someone from the Gas Board arrives. Remember that pets and small children are more quickly adversely affected by gas and other fumes than adults: make sure that they have plenty of fresh air.

GOING TO BED

The chance of a fatality in a home fire is greatly increased at night because of the possibility of asphyxiation by smoke and the difficulty of escaping in time.

1 Make sure that cigarettes and fires are completely extinguished, and nothing inflammable is left in ashtrays.

2 Electrical appliances and gas taps should be firmly turned off. Double check the oven and grill.

3 Do not smoke in bed. Cigarettes, matches and lighters cause about 1 in 10 accidental fires in the home and they account for nearly 40 per cent of deaths in such fires.

4 Always follow the manufacturer's instructions scrupulously when using electric blankets. Never use an overblanket beneath you, nor an underblanket on top of you, unless the manufacturer's instructions specifically state that you can do so. Always switch off the blanket *as you get into bed*, unless it is the type that is designed to be left on for the night. Avoid the temptation of turning it off *after* you get into bed: the chances of dozing off and forgetting to switch off the blanket are too high.

5 Always have all your electric blankets serviced every other year.

6 Before you buy an electric blanket, make sure that it conforms to BS 3456.

7 If you suspect that anything is wrong with the blanket, do not use it. Have it checked and repaired before you use it again.

8 If, as you are about to go to sleep, you think you can smell smoke or burning, don't ignore it or think that you may be imagining it. Investigate it as described below.

SUSPECTING FIRE

If your smoke detector bleeps or if you suspect the outbreak of a fire at night, keep in mind that your priority is to get everyone out of the house before it is too late.

If you suspect the fire to be in a room and the door is shut, do not open it. Instead, run your hand around the top of the frame. If it is hot, do NOT open the door. Alert everyone, open the front door and, provided that there is time, dial 999 for the fire brigade. If there is no time, use a neighbour's telephone.

If you are prevented by intense heat or smoke from getting down the stairs, dial 999 for the fire brigade and then try to alert the attention of neighbours to help you with ladders. Never use a lift in such a situation. If this fails and the fire brigade has not arrived, and smoke and/or flame is appearing around the door frame – which must of course be kept shut in order to retard and delay its spread – you must make up your mind to leave by the window. Don't delay: if you have something in the room that would help to soften your landing, throw it out of the window. Blankets and duvets could be useful. Ideally, get out feet first and lower yourself to the full length of your arms before dropping.

Alternatively, if you judge that you are able to negotiate the stairs and get out in time, then quickly put on slippers or shoes and dressing gown and wrap a towel or jersey around your head. This vital part of fire drill is to enable you to pass by flame and reduce the possibility of burns. If the clothing catches light, throw it off the minute you are outside. Provided that you escape unscathed and merely shocked, clothing will keep you warm and help to reduce the effects of shock.

If you have to go through a smoky room, crouch down. The closer to the floor you are, the cooler it will be and the easier for you to breathe.

If you remember, close any doors behind you as this helps to slow down the spread of the fire, because fire needs oxygen to sustain it.

Do not, under any circumstances whatsoever, either hesitate, dither or attempt to collect together things that you would not like to lose. This could cost you your life.

FIRE ESCAPE ROUTES

This is something that you should give thought to with the rest of the family, so that each of you knows the quickest way to escape from the house, no matter where any one of you is at the time, and where the keys are kept, both for doors and windows.

You should determine which route is the quickest from each room.

Fire Escape Routes

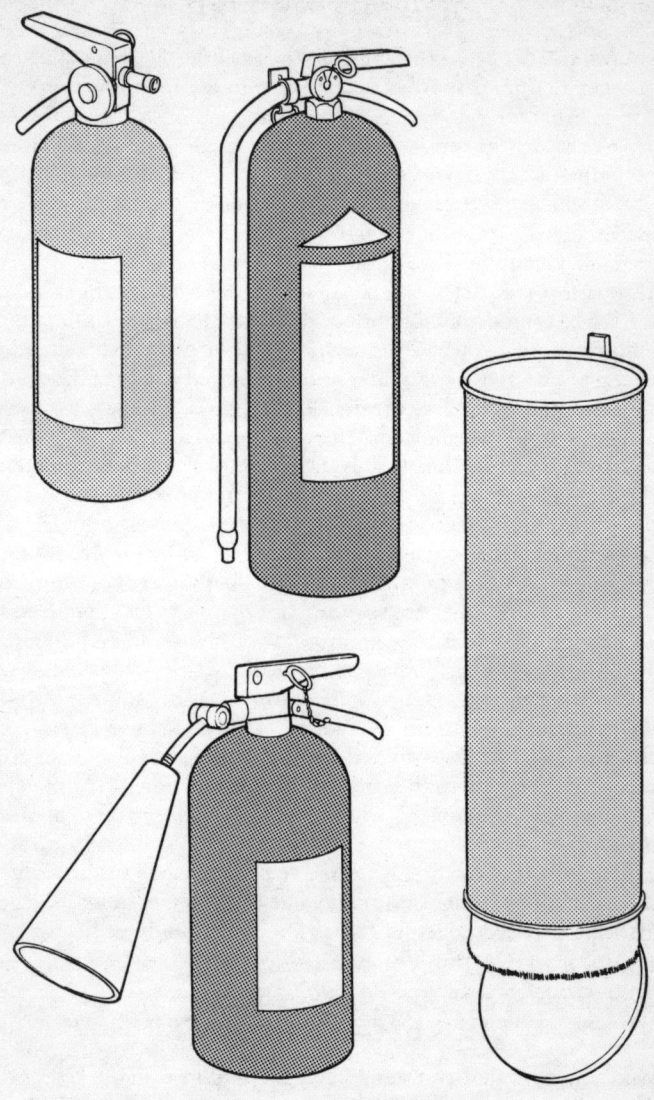

Common types of pressurized gas, water and carbon dioxide fire extinguisher, and a fire blanket. Consult the manufacturer for your particular needs.

Fire Escape Routes · Firefighting

You should also decide which route you would have to take if the stairs could not be used. You should make sure that keys for doors and windows are accessible and that everyone in the house knows exactly where they are. Do not keep upstairs window locks downstairs.

If you live in a flat, especially if it is on an upper floor, pay particular attention to fire escapes. Remember never to use a lift when there is a fire in a building: always take the stairs or the fire escape.

If the building you live in has a fire escape, make sure that you and everyone else in the household knows where the keys are kept. It will be no use to you to know that the keys are kept downstairs by the caretaker if you live on an upper floor. The fire escape should be kept clean and clear of any rubbish that could impede your escape. It should be brushed clear of any snow in the winter.

If there are any windows, however small, or skylights that are at present secured with bars or grilles, consider the possibility of replacing this type of burglar deterrent with good quality locks, as described in Chapters 5, 6 and 7. Should a fire break out, and you were unable to reach the front door, you would have to leave your home by one of the windows, so there should be easy access.

Lastly, think of your pets in the event of a fire breaking out when you are not there. Ideally, cats should have access to a catflap. This does not undermine your security in the context of burglary and could save your cat's life. Clearly, it is not possible to ensure the same security for a dog: the size of emergency access required for a dog would be large enough to admit a burglar. Caged pets would be similarly trapped. There is all the more reason, therefore, to pay meticulous attention to the fire hazards in your home as described earlier in the chapter so that none of you ever have to experience this type of ordeal.

FIREFIGHTING

Your priority is to make sure that you and your family escape a burning building. Heroics can cost life.

If a fire breaks out in one of the rooms in your home and the room is already full of smoke or you can see flames, leave your home straightaway, having alerted the rest of the household. If a fire breaks out in a living room, particularly if it contains modern foam-upholstered furniture, the smoke may contain the poisonous fumes of hydrogen cyanide which can kill in seconds.

New regulations apply to foam upholstered furniture from 1989, but it can be assumed that many households will be furnished for years after that date with the sort of foam upholstered sofas and chairs that,

Firefighting

once ignited, quickly prove fatal. It can also be assumed that the January and July sales, before this type of furniture is finally outlawed, will contain tempting 'bargains' at very low prices to enable shops and manufacturers to clear their stock. You should assume, therefore, that this type of furniture could well be around, if not in your own home, then elsewhere for many years to come.

In the event of a small fire breaking out, you may be able to fight it with a hand fire extinguisher. If a pan of boiling fat catches fire in the kitchen, there may be a chance of smothering it with a fire blanket, provided that the blanket is close at hand. With any small fire, however, you must make your priority the safe evacuation of yourself and your family.

If your clothes catch fire, roll on the floor to extinguish the flames or have someone roll you in blankets, rugs or a thick coat to smother the flames. If you see someone with their clothes alight, quickly roll them in blankets or anything that is to hand: speed is of the essence.

Lastly, remember *never* to fight an electrical fire with water and *never* to use an extinguisher on a fat pan fire.

If there is any question of not being able to extinguish the fire very swiftly, get out and dial 999 for the fire brigade.

·4·

AWAY ON HOLIDAY

The first thing to remember when you are planning a holiday and want to prevent the possibility of a burglary while you are away is: Don't Tell Anyone.

Cities tend to be rather more anonymous and it is easier in general to keep a secret, but nevertheless be very wary about whom you tell that you will be away for a fortnight. In smaller communities, of course, such as small towns and villages, it is practically impossible to keep this sort of information quiet. People will notice that you are away and some people will have to be told anyway, such as the newsagent and daily help.

While you are planning home security for your forthcoming absence, it is worth re-reading Chapter 2 as this shows you how not to advertise the fact that you are away. However, for an absence of more than a few hours, there are several additional precautions to be taken to increase security.

Firstly, make sure that all foreseeable deliveries are cancelled: these may include milk, newspapers, laundry, for example.

If you have a friendly neighbour close by, it would be worth asking him or her to keep an eye on the house, perhaps in the morning if possible, and make sure that any post or leaflets are pushed right through the letterbox. If you live in a grubby inner city area, where hamburger cartons are a nightly hazard, perhaps these could be removed so that the house does not look neglected – a sure sign the owner is away.

If you have an outside telephone bell, make sure that it is switched off or connected to an Ansaphone so that it does not alert passers-by with hostile intentions to the fact that there is no one there. Your Ansaphone message must on no account declare, 'I'm away for a fortnight but back on 24th . . .' Your message should either say that you are in a meeting and will return the call as soon as possible; or, better still arrange with a friend or colleague that the Ansaphone refers callers

▶ *Away on Holiday*

to their number with the message. 'You can get me on 555 6677 at the moment'. They then establish that the call is genuine and tell the caller you will telephone them upon your return from holiday.

It would be a wise precaution to deposit any small valuables, notably jewelry, with your bank. No matter where you hide it in the house, an experienced thief, given enough time, will find it. A hiding place that you may consider wonderfully devious serves to delay a burglar somewhat, but the chances are he will find it in the end.

Never arrange to have any jobs done in the house while you are away unless you are absolutely sure that the person who is to do them has impeccable credentials and that he is not likely to subcontract the job to someone who may be a complete stranger as far as you are concerned.

Be wary, too, of people you employ regularly but not frequently, such as window cleaners. If they telephone to arrange a date with you during the time that you will be away, just say 'Oh, I'm not sure that will be convenient – what about this week?' or 'Perhaps I could give you a ring in a week or two'.

Take a look outside and around and make sure that the place looks reasonably cared for. Do cut the lawn just before you go away: very long grass in the summer often signifies that the owner is away.

Don't put the dustbins out just before you go away if you know that the dustmen always make a mess, scattering litter around and leaving the lids off the bins. Better to invest in some black sacks on your return.

If you have pets, in particular a cat or any caged animals, you will probably have arranged to have a neighbour come in and feed them. If this is the case, the neighbour will be able to remove the tell-tale signs of the absence, such as leaflets stuck through the letterbox and litter close to the house. And if there is snow on the ground, her visits will help to plough it up a little so that the path to your door does not appear to be unused.

AUTOMATIC LIGHTS

One of the best ways of making your home appear to be occupied at night is to invest in automatic lights, which can be fitted by a competent electrician. Have him fit perhaps two downstairs – one for the kitchen and one for a living room – to be set to come on just before dusk and go out at the time that you would normally go to bed. Have him fit at least one more in a bedroom, ideally connected to a bedside light so that it looks as if you are reading in bed, and have that set for about a couple of hours at around your normal bedtime. Be wise about

Automatic Lights · Getting Ready to Leave

whom you employ to do this: don't choose someone from the local paper (successful workmen seldom have to advertise). Ask the person that has seen to your electrical problems in the past to do it, or a competent friend or, failing both of those, a small security firm (who will be cheaper than a large security firm). You should always aim for personal recommendation when choosing a security firm or, failing that, they should be on the approved list held by your local Crime Prevention Officer at your local police station. An alternative, and cheaper option, is to buy two or three electrical time switches and plug table lamps into these, so that it seems to the casual burglar as if several rooms are occupied.

Automatic lights fitted outside, which come on as anyone crosses their beam, can also be most effective in scaring off the opportunist intruder. Unfortunately, these lights will also be activated as animals pass within their arc but it is unlikely that this would negate their effectiveness as a first stop in home security. (Apart from their usefulness as a security measure, they are undoubtedly convenient for you and other members of the family when you come home in the dark.)

GETTING READY TO LEAVE

As it nears the point of your departure, don't do anything really silly like openly packing your car the evening before and then leaving it overnight, fully laden, for everyone to see. Not only are you risking on-the-spot theft but you have also issued a notice of 12 hours' duration

An open invitation for burglars: don't leave your car fully packed outside your house just before your holiday.

Getting Ready to Leave

that you are about to go away. Pack the car as quickly as possible just before you are due to leave and have everything that you intend to pack just inside the front door to cut down on the time that it takes you.

If you have no option but to take a cab to the nearest station, such as if you have an early flight to catch, there is no need to tell the driver that you are leaving the country for a few weeks. Let him think you are going on a day trip to Eastbourne or Manchester (just make sure that your pretended destination has some connection with the station he has delivered you to) and refrain from labelling your luggage 'Heraklion' until you are on the next stage of your journey.

And now that you've done everything that you reasonably can, don't give another thought to home. Have a good holiday!

·5·

DOORSTOPS

Some 38 per cent of burglaries are carried out by breaking in through a door – or in some cases, by simply opening it. In other words, more than 1 in 3 burglars find that they can get into a flat or house through the front door or through a back or side door. This is obviously something that could be prevented with a small investment.

THE FRONT DOOR

You should look first at the construction of the door and the frame around it. It will be no use fitting security locks or any other device if the door is not strong enough to withstand a determined shoulder to it. If you are not sure whether all your external doors are robust enough for good security, consult your local Crime Prevention Officer at your local police station and a good, reliable builder.

Do not make the assumption that if a door is wooden, it must be stronger than a glass one, for example. This is not necessarily so. Glass is available in burglar-resistant strengths – indeed, in bullet-proof strengths; if a wooden door is of panel construction, however, this is comparatively simple to break through and makes less noise than the sound of breaking glass. A thin door, in addition, can be further weakened by cutting into it and into the frame to fit a heavy security lock. So, do satisfy yourself first about the construction of each external door: this applies equally to front door, side doors, back doors, French windows and patio doors. Your local Crime Prevention Officer will be familiar with the different types of high security locking devices available for each.

The next thing to check is that there is no other way of getting in through the door. You letterbox should be critically assessed: it is quite surprising what even the most inexperienced thief is capable of. He may be able to slide his arm through the letterbox and up towards the lock and undo it if the box is more than 5 cm (2 in) deep: it may not sound possible but, believe me, it has been done many times. One of the ways to prevent this is to affix a bottomless letter cage to the letterbox. The cage should ideally be bottomless so that a potential burglar does not instead steal your mail. You may also decide to move

The Front Door

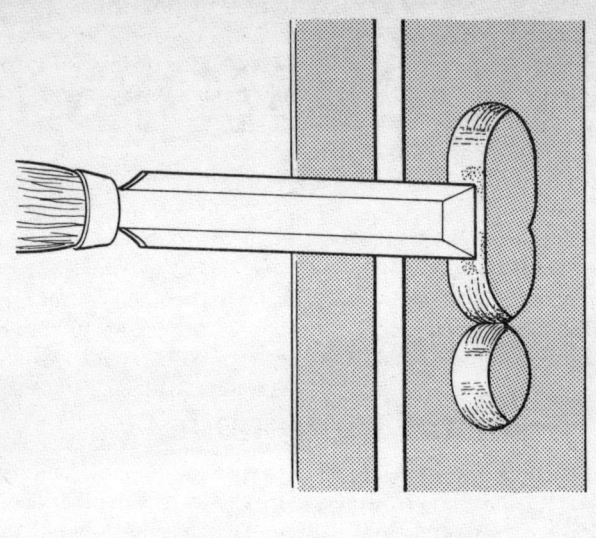

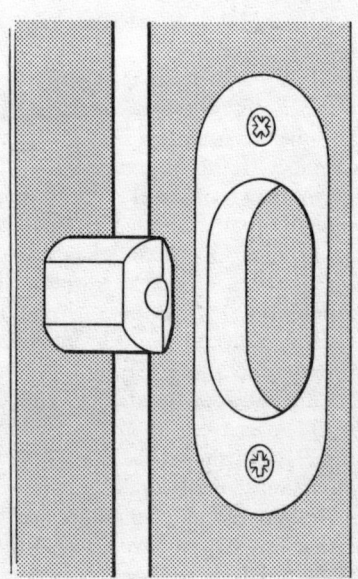

Hinge bolts are easily fitted and will prevent doors being lifted off their hinges. Invisible from the outside, they give an added dimension of security.

The Front Door

the lock on the door, but in general this is not to be recommended because it means that there will be a second incision into the door and the frame and the original incision in both door and frame will need to be filled, thus creating a weak spot.

Next, you should be sure that the hinges of the door are sturdy. This is frequently the weak spot. Your Crime Prevention Officer may advise you to have hinge bolts fitted, in which case you should fit two, one near each existing hinge, as shown in the diagram.

Now that the door and frame are strengthened for security requirements, you should turn your attention to the lock. It is best to use either a five lever security mortise deadlock or the ten lever variation. These locks are difficult to pick and in the case of Ingersoll ten lever locks, for example, you cannot get a duplicate cut except by sending off to the manufacturer who will have registered your details at the time of purchase of the original lock. Simple latches, known as nightlatches, that you can force with a plastic credit card are no deterrent to a thief and should either be added to, in the form of a second lock, or replaced.

The type of door and the way in which it is set into the frame will determine which of the various locks on the market is the best for you. It is recommended that you take expert advice on this from your local Crime Prevention Officer and then have a reputable locksmith or security firm fit it. The setting of a lock is a skilled job and should not be regarded as a DIY task.

The next stage, however, can be carried out by a competent handyperson, and that is to fit a device which allows you to identify a caller without actually admitting them before you are sure of who it is. This device could take the form of a peephole for wooden doors (properly know as door viewers or spyholes); a door chain or limiter; or an entryphone. Door viewers are simple, efficient and easy to fit (*see* diagram). Chains in various finishes and strengths are sold at hardware shops but it is advisable to buy one made by any well-known security company, such as Chubb, so that it is strong enough to withstand an attempted break in. A door limiter serves the same purpose but is more robust. Devices such as chains and spyholes are designed for your personal security at home and to prevent a bogus caller getting a foot in the door: you should use them each time you open the door even if you happen to be expecting someone you know – it might not be them.

Entryphones are a little more complex to fit but very convenient, as you can fit a receiver both at ground floor levels and upper floor levels, which means you do not have to run downstairs only to find it is a door

The Front Door · The Back Door

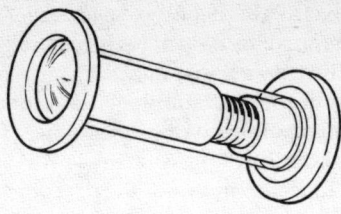

A simple doorviewer can be easily fitted in most front doors.

to door salesman, a religious zealot or someone with more hostile intent. Any competent electrician can fit such a device.

Lastly, you may wish to add a couple of strong steel bolts, but remember these add security only when you are at home. You should not compensate for the deficiency of the main lock by fitting bolts, which will not of course be in use when you are out – and you are many times more likely to be burgled when you are out than when you are in.

When you lock yourself into a building, particularly at night, for example, you should give some thought to how you would get out in the event of a fire. If a fire started in the middle of the night in the sitting room, for example, and you habitually kept the key for the mortise deadlock on the sitting room table when you were in, you would be effectively locked in. Your ground floor windows should be locked (*see next chapter*) and if you were unable to find the key for them in seconds, you would have no alternative but to jump from an upper storey window. Your keys, then, should be kept near you and put with anything else that you might place on your bedside table late at night, such as a watch or spectacles.

Some people say that a barking dog at the door is all the security you need and this may indeed be true of large dogs who are in residence. However, many burglaries have been committed in the presence of dogs, who tend by nature to be affectionate. You must also remember that dogs, especially large dogs, need to be taken out three times a day ... thus regularly relinquishing their duties as guard dogs.

THE BACK DOOR

This is no less vulnerable than the front door. The burglar does not always observe the social niceties of calling at the front door first. You should assess the strength of the back or side door just as critically as the

The Back Door

front door. It may help to bear in mind that of the 38 per cent of burglaries carried out by entry through a door, 20 per cent occurred through the front door and the rest, 18 per cent, were through a side or back door. Nearly 1 in 5 burglars get into a private house, therefore, by the simple expedient of walking round the house or flat and locating what is often an ordinary door with no more than a lock that has been designed for an internal door.

Key operated bolts, also known as mortise security bolts, are useful additions for increasing your security at the back or side door. Go for a well known make, such as Chubb or Banham, and make sure that they are neatly fitted. The advantage of these locks is that they are visible only on the inside – but of course can only be used from the inside.

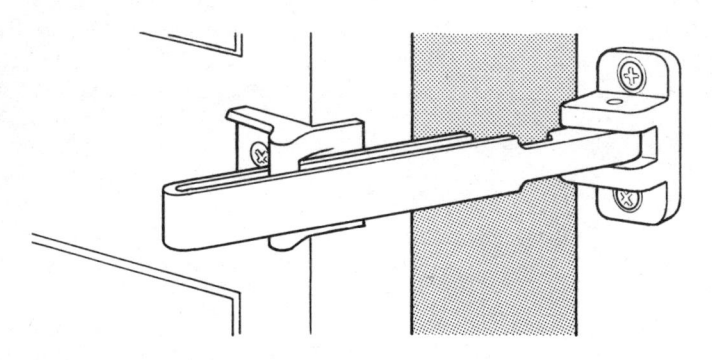

A door limiter allows you to talk with callers safely until you identify them.

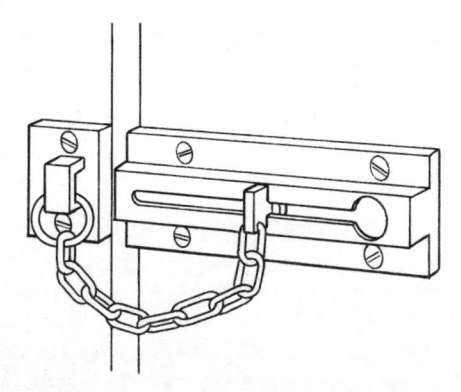

A door chain should be sturdy and of a well-known make.

The Back Door · Catflaps · Patio Doors

There is no sign of them on the outside of the door which means that they cannot be tampered with. You could, if you wished, have them fitted to the front door, but they would increase your security only when you were in. They can also be fitted to windows.

CATFLAPS

Be sure not to leave the door open for the cat while you pop upstairs for an hour or two: because this is convenient for a burglar as well. If there is a reason why you cannot fit a catflap, you will have to put the cat out, lock up and go back and let him in a little later. If you should fit a catflap, make sure that it is no bigger than those commercially available. Anything on the large side, such as would do for a dog's comings and goings, would be equally handy for a thief. (That may sound extraordinary but it has been known!)

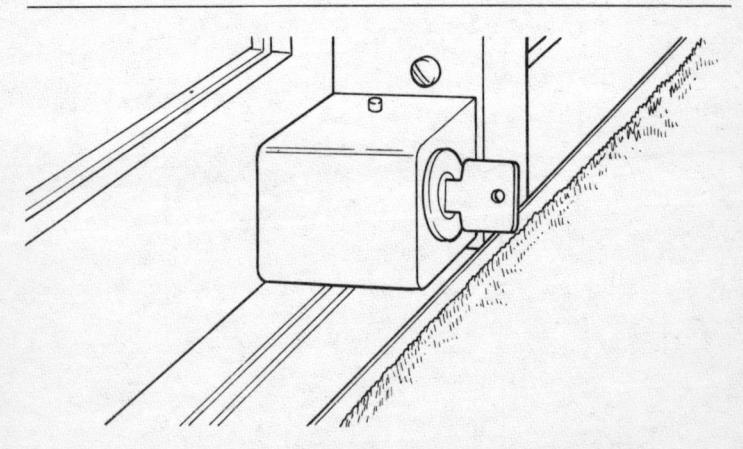

Specialist patio locks can be fitted to give adequate security for glass doors.

PATIO DOORS

These may look vulnerable at first sight but, provided they have been fitted by a reputable firm, they are tougher than they look. Your local Crime Prevention Officer will be able to tell you what sort of glass has been fitted and whether there are 2 or 3 thicknesses. He will also be able to advise on the best sort of patio door lock, which should be fitted by a reputable locksmith or security company.

'JUST POPPING OUT'

Even if you live in a terraced house and you intend to be no more than a minute at your neighbour's, *DO* lock up. You may be delayed, she may ask you in or you may forget when you have had a word with her that the house is unlocked and pop down to the shop. For a variety of reasons, 'a minute' may turn into quarter or half an hour before you've remembered that the back door is unlocked and the front door is on the latch. That is sufficient time for a burglar to pick up all your jewelry and a few video cassettes as well.

AN OPEN INVITATION

Despite all the publicity given in recent years to an advancing crime wave, some people still do the things that burglars hope and look for: REMEMBER:

   1 *DON'T* leave your front door key underneath the mat
   2 *DON'T* leave it under a flowerpot
   3 *DON'T* hang it on a string which you can get hold of by putting your hand through the letterbox

Lastly, please remember what was said in Chapter 2 – *never* leave a note on your front door declaring 'Gone out – back in half an hour'.

▶ *Doorstops*

·6·

WINDOW DRESSING

Most types of window can be secured with one of the numerous locking devices currently on the market. One of the great advantages of securing your windows is that the devices can be seen from the outside and this is sometimes enough to deter the opportunist burglar.

Nearly two-thirds of all burglars manage to break in through open or unprotected windows: some 48 per cent make their way in through a window at the back of the house, while a further 6 per cent choose a side window and the last 7 per cent break in through a front window. Although this means that they can easily be seen, an experienced burglar can deal with an unprotected window in a couple of minutes – so all he has to do is take a look up and down the road and if there is no one approaching, he will quickly be into the house.

The most common types of window are sash and casement; there are also transom, fanlight and louvre windows. Patio doors and French windows are classified as doors and you should therefore refer to the previous chapter for information about securing these.

In the same way that the security of a door depends on the intrinsic strength of the door and the frame themselves, so it is with windows. If, for example, the glass is very thin, or it is not securely fixed into the frame, or if the frame is breaking up and either rusting or rotten (depending on whether it is made of metal or wood), no type of window lock will be able to provide the required security. It is essential that the window is a good, firm fit to the frame: the windows of old houses, in particular, will have weathered and it is not unusual to be able to slide something like a screwdriver between window and frame in a bid to force them open.

So, first check the fabric of the window frame and fixing – including the state of the putty.

There are certain sorts of window that are particularly vulnerable to attack. These should, if possible, be avoided or replaced: they include leaded windows (known as leaded lights) and louvre windows. The lead around leaded lights is fairly soft and therefore not difficult to remove; and, because each one is individual, the burglar is not confronted with the hazard of the sound of breaking glass. Louvre windows should never be fitted to ground floor windows as they are undoubtedly vulnerable to burglary: the glass slats can be slid quite easily out of their channels and laid soundlessly upon the ground in a matter of minutes.

It should also be noted that wire reinforced glass (glass with wire mesh running through it) is not particularly robust (nor is it designed to be) and can be kicked in without much difficulty. (This type of glass is intended to retard the spread of fire rather than deter burglars.) Extra strong laminated glass is much stronger and recommended for use of very large windows. It is harder to smash than normal glass and it possesses a further advantage in the context of home safety: its core is plastic and if someone tries to smash it, or if they accidentally fall against it, the pieces stay together rather than collapsing into shards and splinters.

WHAT SORT OF PROTECTION?

Unlike door security, aesthetic considerations have a part to play in securing your windows. A series of bars may seem to be invincible but will do nothing to enhance the appearance of your home; there is, furthermore, the question of your escape in the event of a fire. I would not recommend any fixed bars or decorative grills since you would be trapped should fire break out. However, what are known as telescopic gates, a movable grille, would be comparatively safe, if not particularly aesthetically pleasing when in use. However, since they can be opened and closed, they can be kept open while you are in and closed and locked only at night and while you are out. In high risk situations, such as basements with low-level windows, which cannot be seen from the road, telescopic gates would probably be a worthwhile investment, but would certainly not be cheap. A nicer looking option may be to install solid wooden shutters.

There is a great variety of window locks on the market and before you look at them, you will need to identify the following:

1 the type of window to which the lock is to be fitted

2 what the window is made of: it is most likely to be metal or wood, but could be plastic

3 the width available for fixing a locking device

4 the required finish – a question of aesthetics

☐ Who fits the locks?

When it comes to fitting locking devices, you have several alternatives: a reputable security company such as Chubb, a local locksmith on a personal recommendation or recommendation by your local Crime Prevention Officer, any competent handyman whom you trust and whose work you know is of a good standard, or, lastly, DIY. Doing it yourself may appear to be a soundly priced option, but it must be said that fitting locks to a good and secure standard is a skill and, in this context, the job is not worth doing if it is not done properly. Furthermore, if you use a security company or a locksmith, you can be reasonably sure that they will select the correct device for each of your different windows from the many different ranges on the market. Even the quality and strength of the screws used to fix the device are important, and the length of the screw is of course crucial. Too short and the device will be easy to force open; too long and it will go right through the frame to the other side. If you do fix the locks yourself, buy an extra strong quality of screw and use the non-return type. If you are unable to locate the non-return type, drill out the screw heads when you have fixed the device so that it can be neither removed nor loosened.

SASH WINDOWS

This type of window can be opened from the outside even if it is fitted with a clasp halfway down where the two panes meet. There are, however, a number of efficient locks on the market, designed for either wooden or metal windows. These locks are effective because should a burglar smash the window in order to undo the clasp, he will find that he still cannot get in. He is then faced with smashing out a far larger expanse of glass in order that he can get through the window without cutting himself, and this takes time and makes a lot of noise. It is at this point that the opportunist may well decide that the job is not worth the bother and go elsewhere. If one is fortunate, it may be that the burglar has looked through the window before he smashes it and has observed that it is fitted with locks. In that case he may not even attempt a forced entry.

There are many different types of locking devices for sash windows which include:

1 acorn devices which protrude and restrict movement of wooden sash windows

2 dual screw devices which prevent movement of the sashes by

Sash Windows

A dual screw window lock is useful for sash windows.

screwing them together
   3 sash locks which limit the movement of the sashes
   4 sliding window locks
   5 key operated mortise rack bolts or locks
Some devices allow the window to be set in two positions: fully closed or slightly open. The latter sounds convenient as a selling point, but it should be appreciated that any window that is slightly open, whether locked or not, offers a criminal an easier task and, at first glance certainly, appears to extend an invitation to break in.

Keep keys to window locks like this nearby in case of fire.

CASEMENT WINDOWS

As there are for sash windows, there are also a number of different locking devices that are suitable for casement windows. You should first determine whether your frames are metal or wooden, and, as with all security devices, have an expert advise you if possible on the final selection.

Should someone attempt a forced entry, he will probably attempt to force the window open; when he finds that this is impossible, he may smash the pane in order to release the casement window handle and stay. He will then find that the window still does not open and it is at this point that he may well decide the job is becoming too protracted and the associated risk thus too high.

Devices include:

1 casement locks which fasten the casement and the frame together
2 screw/stops fixed to the window stays which prevent them being lifted and the windows thus opened
3 cockspur stops to prevent the handle of the window being raised
4 locking bolts for fastening casement or transom windows to their frames
5 mortise rack bolts which fasten wooden casements to their frames
6 locking devices that are integral parts of the window handles, known as substitute catches.

VALUE FOR MONEY

When you make your choice as to what sort of device to fit, be guided not only by at least two different and independent experts but by price, too. It is true that a cheap device may be effective but it is also true that tougher, better quality and better designed devices are likely to reflect their superiority in a higher price. It is essential to buy the best that you can afford, simply because windows are so vulnerable to attack. You cannot make them impregnable (except by fitting bars or grilles) and you must therefore make the job of breaking and entering as difficult and as time-consuming as you possibly can.

KEY SECURITY

You should also take into account the fact that just as all these devices are widely available at hardware and DIY stores, so too are the keys that operate them. A burglar may well carry some of the common keys and you should consider therefore whether it is worth choosing locks or

Key Security · Long-Term Vigilance

devices that are operated either by unique keys or by differing keys. If you buy from a security company, you will be offered the option of unique security keys for your locking devices; you are registered as the owner and no one else can obtain duplicates. They cannot be replicated at a high street key-cutting shop. Differing keys means that you are buying a system that is operated by a certain key; the same key will be able to open some, but not all, other locking devices of the same type. The cheapest option is to buy devices that are operated by common keys; in other words, that key will open every device of that type.

LONG-TERM VIGILANCE

Security experts agree that many people give little thought to matters of security until they are burgled. They may tighten up their security after a burglary, but it is another well-known fact that people tend to relax their vigilance within a year or so of being burgled. This is particularly relevant in the context of windows and especially so in the summer. Few people would feel, especially after being burgled, that it was too much trouble to lock back and front doors properly. However, faced with locking all the windows on a summer's day just for the sake of a short trip to the shops, many people decide to chance it, leaving them unlocked even though they have made the investment in good security. If you have a burglar alarm, as an additional level of security, leaving the windows open may not seem such a serious risk; if you do not, simply remind yourself that well over half of all burglaries are committed by the simple expedient of getting through a window. If your windows are either open or unprotected you are *more* likely to be burgled than if you left the front door open.

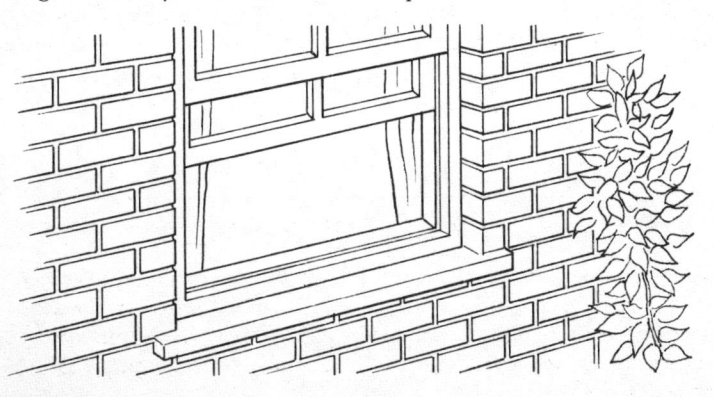

WINDOW SHOPPING

One last word of warning: avoid leaving valuable or desirable items within easy sight of the street for burglars to do their window shopping. Metropolitan Police in South London conducted a door to door campaign in 1987 to alert householders that their TV/video/stereo could be seen easily through the window and to advise them to move it away from a direct line of sight from the street. When you put the lights on at night, be sure to draw the curtains as you are otherwise providing a spotlit array of goods, and affording a potential burglar a perfect opportunity for casing the joint and deciding whether it is worth breaking and entering the following day.

·7·

ILLEGAL ENTRY

Burglary is more often than not associated with breaking and entering through a door or window. There are, however, other means of entering a house illegally. Of 100 burglaries one will have involved the burglar gaining entry using a less orthodox method. The weak spot might be the roof, particularly in the case of roof hatches (common in terraced houses), skylights, cellars and integral garages which lead straight into the house. The downpipes running from the house gutters to the ground afford a burglar a particular advantage which you can eradicate. The other favoured method of entering a house illegally is to pretend to be someone who would normally be allowed access without question: they are known as bogus traders/callers.

Before you dismiss the idea that someone will break in other than through a door or window and take heart from the fact that one in 100 is not so very many, bear these two things in mind: given that over 500,000 house burglaries are committed in Great Britain each year, no less than 5,000 burglaries are staged using one of the more unusual ways of entry. I know of one elderly lady living in Brixton, South London, who has been broken into three times in two years – through the roof hatch. The house was occupied on all three occasions, each of which took place during the night.

ROOF HATCHES

A row of terraced houses, each with an unprotected roof hatch, offers an energetic burglar considerable scope. Although he will be unable to take away furniture or large and bulky items such as television sets, he will nevertheless probably make a good picking from small antique objects, cash and jewelry, all of which can be stored safely in his pockets. It is not unknown for a burglar to go from one house to another in this situation, leaving one house by the roof hatch exit and

Roof Hatches

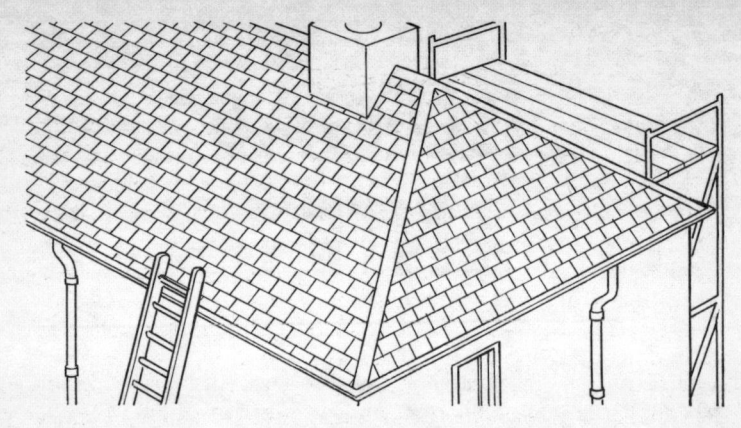

entering the house next door by the adjacent roof hatch.

You should consider both internal and external security in an attempt to make sure that this does not happen to you. The roof hatch should be firmly secured from the inside, so firmly that it can withstand a man's weight jumping on it. Thick, sturdy 30 cm (12 in) bolts, one each side of the access flap, fixed with extra strong screws of the correct length could be one solution; another would be to lock the access flap into its frame with a window locking device such as mortise bolts. Clearly, you should not fix bars as you should be able to gain access to the roof for repairs and maintenance and, as an emergency measure in the event of fire.

Your second line of defence, looking at the problem internally, should be the loft access hatch. This should be fixed just as securely as that to the roof, so that even if a burglar succeeded in breaking and entering through the roof, he is then faced with a further delay and the additional hazard of making sufficient noise to wake up the household if the crime is committed at night.

Looking at the house externally, the obvious routes to the roof include:

1 climbing one of the downpipes
2 clambering up from a flat roof
3 negotiating building scaffolding
4 using a convenient ladder, such as might be found in the garage.

There is not a great deal that one can do about flat roofs or building scaffolding except to make sure that all points of entry, notably windows and roof hatches, are well and truly secured. Ladders should never be left outside – not even for half an hour while you go out – and if kept in a garage or other outhouse, they should be securely locked up (*see also Chapter 9: External Forces*).

DOWNPIPES

An experienced cat burglar views a good solid downpipe (particularly those made of cast iron rather than lightweight plastic) as useful as a ladder might be to the rest of us. The police make several recommendations that will help prevent burglars making use of downpipes to enter either through windows or roof hatches. These include:

1 filling the space between downpipe and wall with mortar so that it is impossible to get a handgrip upon the pipe

2 fitting the downpipes with 5-spiked collars at regular intervals

3 encasing the downpipes with barbed wire from about 2 m (6 ft 6 in) up

4 painting the downpipes with special anti-climb paint. This is paint that sets only superficially, forming an external skin. The paint beneath does not dry out, so that if someone touches it and breaks the skin, they will find themselves grappling with a wet and slippery downpipe. However, if you do decide to use this, you should warn the window cleaner, the person who cleans out your gutters, any building or roofing contractor and, in the event of your moving, the new owner. If you use any of the above methods, which are likely to inflict harm on an intruder, you should put up a warning notice otherwise you can face prosecution under the Householders' Liabilities Act.

SKYLIGHTS

Unlike windows which might have to be used as a means of escape in the event of a house fire, skylights are usually placed in such a position that they could not be used for such a purpose. If this is the case, they can be safely barred or fitted with a fixed decorative grille. If you use bars, you should be guided by your local Crime Prevention Officer as to the correct spacing for the size and shape of the skylight. On the other hand, if it is obvious that the skylight is so placed that it could be used as a window, a safer option would be to treat it as such and fit it with sturdy locking devices. If it is fitted with wire reinforced mesh glass, you should also consider the possibility of replacing it with a more robust laminate.

CELLARS

Your cellar may be fitted with a small dark and dusty window which yields little light and which you may not have considered as an ideal weak spot for a burglar to choose. You may well think of the cellar as

▶ *Illegal Entry*

securely below ground and the ideal place to store valuables when you are away. However, small, dark and dusty windows, particularly at sub-ground level and therefore not easily visible from the street, present a most convenient point of entry for a burglar. You should treat any such window as a normal window and secure it as well as all the others (*see* Chapter 6). If the cellar is fitted with an external door, or a coal hatch, these too should be checked for a good firm fit and securely locked and/or bolted (*see Chapter 5: Doorstops*). Any grating should be secured with a substantial chain and padlock. You may also consider the possibility of bricking up any unused openings, notably coal hatches and gratings.

BLIND SPOTS

If you have an integral garage leading straight into the house, you may tend to think of it as 'the garage' rather than part of the house. Not only is it part of the house but it is in fact very vulnerable to break in: it houses useful equipment for house-breaking (tools) and valuables of the sort that some burglars specialize in (cars, lawnmowers, hedge trimmers and chainsaws). So, when you evaluate the total security of your house, make sure you don't overlook any of its elements. These include integral garages, integral utility rooms and boiler houses, extensions, and conservatories.

It is said that the larger the pane of glass, the less likely it is to be broken by a burglar because it will make a lot of noise and possibly attract unwelcome attention. However, it is also true that, although additions are often made almost totally of glass, they are also peculiarly vulnerable to attack. This can be because they have been attached to the house as an afterthought and the question of security simply has not been considered.

Very large glass structures, it must be said, are probably best protected by a burglar alarm (*see* next chapter). If you decide against this, you should at least ensure that the glass is a sturdy laminate and that locks are fitted wherever possible and practicable. Telescopic gates are a further possibility in a high risk situation, but are an option that is neither inexpensive nor aesthetically pleasing.

BOGUS TRADERS

A burglar may come to your front door for any one of a number of motives. He may wish to establish the kind of person the owner is and whether, from a superficial viewing, they are likely to possess valuable

Bogus Traders

or saleable objects. He may attempt to look over the house – casing the joint, as it is known in criminal parlance – under the guise of reading a meter or some other excuse. He may simply seek to divert your attention while an accomplice looks round the back of the house. He may have been on the point of committing a burglary there and then – until he discovered that there was someone in the house. Or, worst of all, he may attempt a forcible entry.

For all these reasons, your front door should be protected as described in *Chapter 5* either with a chain, a limiter or a spyhole. You *must* establish that any caller is absolutely genuine; and you should not be embarrassed to do this. If you remain unconvinced about the identity of the caller, do not under any circumstances open the door or admit him. This also applies to female callers as they may be acting as an accomplice or, indeed, as the primary burglar.

Bogus traders/callers fall into several different categories: there are those who pretend to have some entirely innocent business connected with either your house or yourself and who, if genuine, would normally be admitted without hesitation. These include:

- police
- telephone engineers
- gas board workers
- water board workers
- television rental collectors
- council workmen

There are other callers who explain themselves by offering to do a job of work for you (that you may well not need doing). They may offer to:

- re-tarmac the drive
- repair the roof
- clean the windows
- provide a home security survey
- landscape the garden.

Alternatively, they may ask you to take part in some survey, if they are a more upmarket type of burglar. First of all, never forget that any skilled workman who is any good rarely has to advertise and would certainly not consider touting for business on a door to door basis. Secondly, it is in any case advisable to use only workmen who come to you by recommendation. Thirdly, you must never admit a total stranger to your house.

In the case of the first category of callers, you should ask to see their identification, still keeping the chain on the door. You should look at it

▲ *Illegal Entry*

Bogus Traders

Visitors' identity cards should be checked carefully before you admit strangers to your home.

and read it properly. It should be a proper card, with a photograph of the bearer and a signature; and it will probably be laminated in clear plastic. If you are not sure whether the caller is genuine, or you feel instinctively that there is something fishy about the visitor, do not feel compelled out of politeness to admit them. Simply explain that their visit is not convenient for you at the moment and ask them to return at a later time/date. Then check with their office or headquarters. If the authenticity of the call cannot be verified in this way, you should inform the police immediately as the caller may be about to visit

Bogus Traders

another house in your neighbourhood.

Lastly, if a stranger arrives at your door with what appears to be a genuine need for help, such as:

1 there's been an accident in the street
2 his wife is ill
3 his car has broken down
4 he needs directions

... the rules remain the same. Do not admit a stranger to your house. Tell him/her courteously that you will call an ambulance/a doctor/the police/the local garage or give them the required directions; then close the door, still upon its chain.

▶ *Illegal Entry*

·8·

ALARM BELLS

Most households these days have a car and a stereo system, but it is still the case that most households do not have a burglar alarm. This is surprising because a professionally fitted burglar alarm can save you thousands of pounds in terms of valuables stolen, damage done to property and the loss of your time. The difference is of course that a car is actively and visibly useful, although deteriorating in value all the time; and a stereo, which costs on average the same as a burglar alarm, gives you *active* enjoyment. An alarm is essentially a *passive* device.

No one seems to know how many people have a burglar alarm, but it is clear that those who do are in a minority. Some experts say about 8 per cent of people have an alarm. The National Supervisory Council for Intruder Alarms (NSCIA) are not able to collate figures for all domestic alarms as there are many installers, and of course DIY householders, who are not members of the Council. Of all installations carried out by their own members in 1982, when figures were last issued, some 10.3 per cent were for domestic premises with the vast majority designated for business and commercial premises. Given a steadily increasing crime rate, an equally steady decrease in police resources, the number of installations by non-NSCIA members and the number of home DIY alarms, it is probably the case that the number of home owners electing for this type of security is increasing at a dramatic rate.

Many people are still resistant to the idea of having a burglar alarm fitted for a number of reasons. The first may be expense (an alarm for a four-bedroomed house is unlikely to be less than £500 plus VAT in 1988). The second concerns nuisance value – 'Will it bother the neighbours?' If the alarm is not professionally and correctly fitted, or if it develops persistent faults, it will. The worst aspect of this is that neighbours are first annoyed and then actively hostile to the existence of the alarm. When it goes off, they will suspect a fault rather than a

Alarm Bells · Is It Necessary?

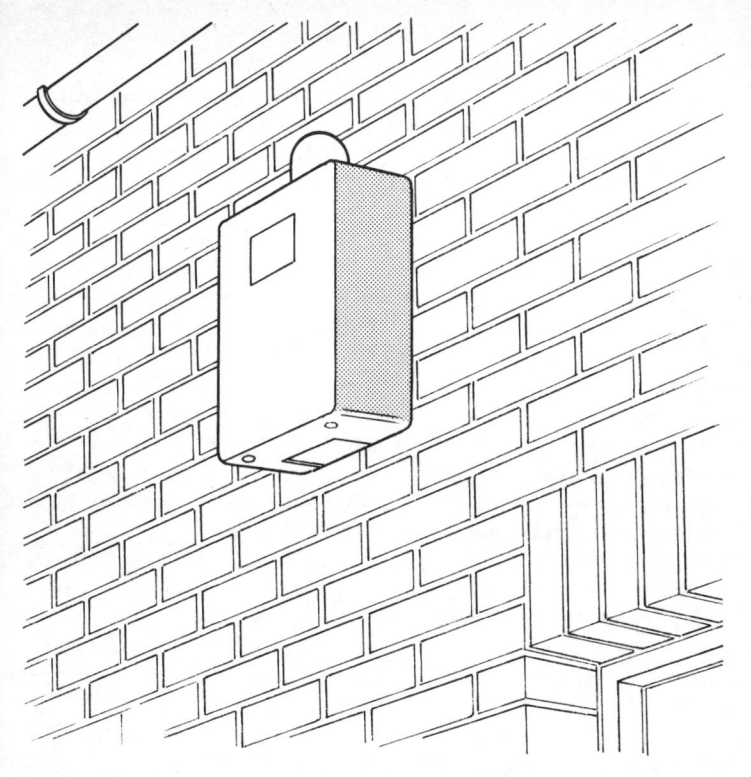

A burglar alarm will offer the most effective deterrent to casual burglars.

true alarm and tend to ignore it. The third area of resistance concerns whether an alarm is actually necessary; and, as part of that question, what good will it do even if it is proven to be necessary?

IS IT NECESSARY?

There are a number of levels of security, as described in Chapter 1. The first concerns your lifestyle and your habits – basically applying good common sense. Level 2 requires you to be a little more ingenious and to create the impression that your home is occupied even when it is not. Level 3 encompasses the elimination of weak spots, the tightening up of physical security and the addition of further physical deterrents to burglary or break in (*see* Chapters 5, 6 and 7). Physical deterrents are

Is it Necessary?

simply that: they do not prevent, they simply deter. They also delay a potential burglar.

One of the main advantages of a burglar alarm is its deterrent value: although some people believe that it serves to advertise that you have something worth stealing, the police and security experts believe that few burglars will continue with a theft once the alarm is triggered and the siren heard. We are concerned here with the type of alarm known as 'audible-only' – in other words, it sounds a noisy siren on being triggered; it does not ring silently at the alarm company's headquarters, alerting them to call the police, who, it is hoped, then turn up and arrest the burglar. Police and security experts believe that the siren is sufficiently panic-inducing and distracting to scare off the potential burglar. It is true, however, that an alarm does not *prevent* burglary any more than door and window locks do: but it is a further deterrent, another hurdle.

Only you can decide whether an alarm is necessary. It depends on a number of factors:

1 how may times you have been burgled before

2 how many valuables you have to protect and whether or not you can afford to lose pictures/jewelry/antiques that cannot be replaced

3 whether you are nervous when alone in the house

4 whether you are nervous in the house at night

5 what kind of area your home is in. Some parts of cities such as London are classified as very high risk. A few years ago one street in South London, for example, experienced 44 burglaries – in just one street. There might only be half a dozen a year in the whole of a rural village.

My own experiences may help you to decide: I lived in a basement flat in Chelsea, West London, for 9 years, between 1975 and 1984. I was burgled five times in the first two years. In 1977 I had a burglar alarm fitted and was not burgled again – although the alarm was triggered numerous times. In 1984 I moved to a house in Camberwell, South London, and had a burglar alarm fitted within weeks of moving in. For the three years that I lived there, I was burgled once and that was when I had gone next door for just eight minutes to feed the cat – and had omitted to put the alarm on. In effect, therefore, the house was never burgled while the alarm was on. A night-time break-in was attempted, but the alarm triggered and the intruder escaped before the police arrived. The alarm was triggered at other times and may have signified attempted break-ins.

It should never be forgotten that the great majority of burglars are opportunists rather than professionals who have targeted your home

Is it Necessary? · Fitting an Alarm

and planned their attack in advance. The opportunist, practically by definition, will not be attracted to the house with a burglar alarm. He may attempt a break-in to see if the alarm is more than merely a dummy bell cover, but at the point that the siren sounds, the majority of opportunist burglars will run.

FITTING AN ALARM

The type of alarm fitted will be more or less determined by who fits it. The amateur DIY alarm systems, probably operated by battery, will be fitted only by householders. Professional types of systems with an audible-only siren can be fitted by large or small security companies, by local electricians or by a competent handyman. None of these people will be able to offer a remote signalling service, in which the alarm, rather than ringing in the house, instead rings at a central station or at the local police station. For anything more complex than an audible-only siren, a security company has to be used.

Each company has its own network of suppliers and manufacturers and its own preferences for the sort of equipment it will fit. For this reason, it is essential that you first of all seek the advice of your local Crime Prevention Officer at your local police station on the question of security of the house in general. You should then obtain estimates from at least 3 different security companies. Each company will send a surveyor to determine the best system for you and will specify where each part of the system is to be installed (notably, alarm panel, external bell/siren, magnetic contacts, detectors).

You should question each surveyor closely and ask him why he has chosen this system rather than that and this position rather than another. If he cannot give intelligent responses to your questions, do

▶ *Alarm Bells*

not use his company and obtain an estimate from a fourth company to replace his. You should also determine, for your own convenience, the extent of upheaval during installation – carpets and floorboards may need to be taken up and walls will probably have to be drilled through, creating dust and mess. Lastly, you should make some attempt to determine how effective the company's back-up system is. While you are obtaining the different estimates for comparison, make a few calls to the company's offices late in the evening and on a Sunday afternoon to see how quickly the telephone is answered (if at all, in some cases) and what you are told when it is answered. If you are informed by an answering machine that your call will be returned the following morning or on Monday morning, you should not use that company and seek an alternative. If your call is answered personally, explain to the person what you are doing, establish where their engineer is and how long it would take him to reach your house had there been a need for a genuine callout. Ascertain, too, whether the engineers have bleeps. If any of the answers are less than satisfactory, go elsewhere.

You are now in a slightly better position to judge which company would be the best to use: if you have a distinct preference for one company over another but they have omitted a feature that is included on the specifications of one of the other companies, ask the one of your choice if it can be included and what their opinion is of the additional feature.

Before you make your final decision, check that the company you wish to use are intending to fit equipment that conforms to British Standards 4737. Be sure to pay no more than a deposit before you are fully satisfied with the installation and functioning of the alarm and confident that you understand it. Do not settle the bill in full before the system has been installed for a week or two to ensure that any teething problems are settled promptly by the company.

There are advantages and disadvantages of each alarm system and it is wise to be familiar with these before an alarm company's surveyor comes to your house to plan your system. The simplest systems, coming into the DIY category, comprise magnetic contacts, pressure mats and silver foil strips containing closed circuit wiring. The next category, and now largely outmoded except in certain outdoor situations, comprises the photoelectric or infra-red beam which, if crossed, triggers the alarm. A third category, which is particularly useful if you have pets, is the method known as inertia sensing which senses any vibration to door or window and then triggers the alarm. The remaining, and most common systems, are described as volumetric systems, with detectors that measure space in one way or another. If

Fitting an Alarm · Doing it Yourself

the characteristics of the measured space alter – as they would if someone stepped into the room – the alarm is activated. Such systems can be divided into three categories: passive infra-red, microwave and ultrasonic. Lastly, the newest development is the wireless radio alarm which works similarly to passive infra-red but has dispensed with the need for wiring to run round the entire house.

DOING IT YOURSELF

You can buy alarm systems from hardware and DIY stores to install yourself at a much lower cost than having a security company advise, supply and fit. Most are battery operated, so you would have to check the life of the batteries at frequent and regular intervals. The DIY systems are not very sophisticated, but in a low risk situation may be adequate to give you some protection and peace of mind.

The DIY systems usually comprise a system of magnetic door contacts and pressure mats. Magnetic door contacts have been on the security market for a long time now and are undoubtedly reliable and effective. If professionally fitted, however, and recessed as to be virtually invisible, they are even better than the DIY types which tend to be surface mounted. Magnetic contacts, often known as reeds, can be sited on doors/door frames and windows/window frames. When they are closed, the magnetic contacts are in contact with one another: if the alarm is on, once the contact is broken, by the door or window being opened, the alarm is activated.

The disadvantage of magnetic contacts is that they cannot detect breaking glass. So, for example, the burglar may break the window pane, clear the opening of glass and enter. Provided that he does not open the window, separating the window from its frame, the alarm will not trigger. Because of this disadvantage, a system that uses magnetic contacts usually also comprises pressure mats, sited at doors and windows, so that if someone breaks in they will trip the alarm by stepping on the mat. These mats are usually concealed under rugs or fitted carpets. They are hermetically sealed plastic outer covers containing two slim metallic plates, between which lies a layer of perforated sponge or foam rubber. When someone steps upon the mat, the perforated holes compress, allowing the metallic plates to touch each other. This creates an electrical contact which activates the alarm.

Pressure mats possess several disadvantages. Firstly, the rubber can wear out and when this happens a large number of false alarms will be given. Secondly, burglars are very familiar with them and they know

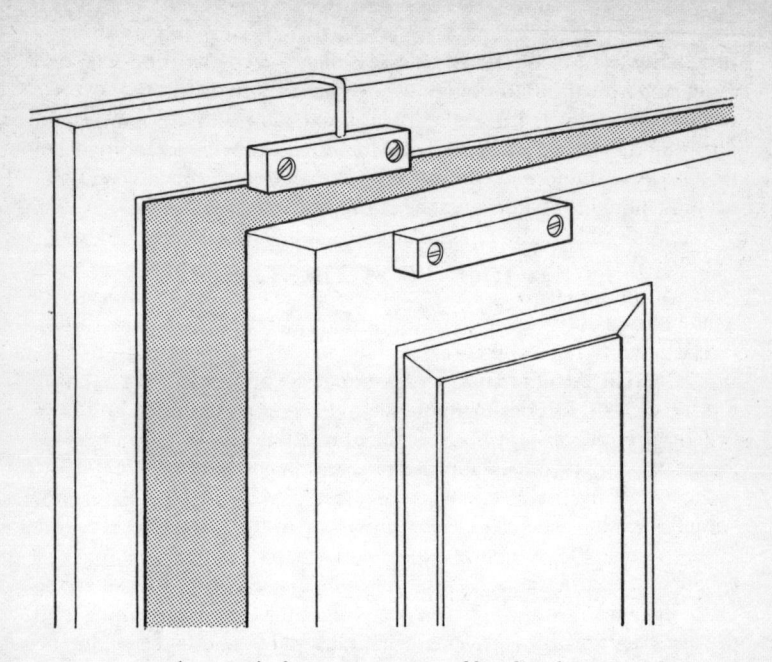

A magnetic door contact system of burglar alarm.

where they are likely to be fitted – beneath French windows, by the door, at the bottom of a flight of stairs, outside the master bedroom (since this is where jewelry is normally kept). Thirdly, any pets have to be kept outside or confined inside one room as the weight of their bodies is sometimes sufficient to activate the alarm. Fourthly, if used without any other system, such as magnetic contacts on doors and windows, they can succeed in activating the alarm only when the intruder is actually in the house; they cannot prevent or deter initial entry.

There are portable alarm systems on the market which normally comprise a movement detector and a loud siren. These small and convenient units can be plugged into a conventional electrical socket. Their disadvantage is that they do not comprise an external bell and they are so unsophisticated that it is unlikely that they would scare off anyone except an inexperienced opportunist, schoolchildren and possibly vandals.

Because neither magnetic contacts nor pressure mats are designed to detect or control the sort of vibration caused by breaking glass, there is a need for an additional element to DIY alarms. This is provided by fitting strips of metallic foil to the glass. These strips comprise a closed circuit system with small terminals fitted on the window frame. When the glass breaks, the foil also breaks, breaking the circuit and thus activating the alarm. This thin foil is delicate, however, and subject to damage by condensation, window cleaners and small children. It should be noted that if part of the foil strip is damaged, the entire strip must be replaced; making a patch repair is unlikely to be effective and is actively discouraged by the NSCIA.

One of the things that causes potential burglars a sense of alarm is the sound or sight of a large dog. Thinking in terms of DIY security, buying a pet and security guard rolled into one may seem like a good idea. However, even the most ferocious dog may succumb to a pound of steak thrown its way. And the dog can do its job only if it is in residence: think of the times you have to walk a dog, or you go on holiday. Dogs should be regarded as security back-ups only if they are in permanent residence and properly trained for the job, as those belonging to the police and security companies are.

PROFESSIONAL SYSTEMS

Moving from the area of low cost DIY systems, there are a number of types of alarm system, each with their inherent advantages and disadvantages.

☐ Photoelectric beams

Devices incorporating invisible rays can be fitted in some situations. They were commonly used in professional burglar alarm systems for houses before the introduction of more comprehensive and sophisticated systems. The ray or beam extends across a room or hallway and works by heat-seeking in the same way as infra-red detectors. Should someone cross the beam, the heat of the body triggers the alarm.

The problems with such beams, which work on a photoelectric or infra-red basis, are manifold: firstly, the location of the beam can be discovered by the burglar if he has the opportunity of reconnoitring the house while the alarm is off. If he is able to do this, he can step over the invisible beam and prevent it triggering the alarm. Once burglar alarm installers appreciated this possibility, it became common practice to fit two beams – one at knee height and one at shoulder height. Into this system was built the added advantage that both rays had to be crossed to trigger the alarm: this meant that a dog or other domestic pet was unable to trigger the alarm. But it also doubled the cost and in a sense lessened security – if the burglar had the intelligence to stoop wherever he suspected beams to be located.

The second and serious disadvantage of such a system was the margin of error. If a beam was sited towards a window, it could extend beyond the area requiring protection. In a city or suburban situation, therefore, it could pick up passing pedestrians or cars with a consequent and unwelcome high rate of false alarms. However, the beam system is useful as a means of covering wide areas or long distances, in an external situation for example. Laser beams are now being used to protect large, vulnerable premises such as warehouses and nuclear installations.

☐ **Inertia sensing**

Because photoelectric beams were never designed to prevent or deter break-ins, but simply to activate the alarm once the intruder was in, vibration or inertia sensors were developed. These can be regarded as a refinement of magnetic door and window contacts. The essential difference is that if the door or window does not shake or move, the magnetic contact does not respond. With vibration sensors, any impact is registered and the sensor sends a signal to the alarm panel, which contains an analyzer. If the impact registered is of such a force to indicate the likelihood of forced entry, the alarm is activated. The analyzer is programmed to discriminate between different frequencies of sound/vibration: it triggers the alarm only when it detects a high frequency at a low amplitude (a hacksaw over an iron bar, for example) or a low frequency at a high amplitude (a hammer and chisel, for example).

The reliability of this system depends absolutely upon the correct setting of the analyzer. It can be set at its most sensitive in a bank vault, for example, where it can be assumed that nothing other than unauthorized entry could trigger it. It can be set in a domestic installation on 'gross attack' – meaning someone has to smash a window or door to set it off. If the system has been set at too sensitive a level in a house, persistent false alarms will occur. The vibration sensors will respond to the vibrations caused by a passing juggernaut, thunder, hail, the builders drilling next door, a train passing along a nearby railway line, a banging cat flap. If you live in a flat, the vibrations caused by very loud music will also trigger your alarm, particularly if the music emanates from the floor above. If, on the other hand, the system is not sensitive enough, it will be useless.

Professional Systems

The advantages of this system is that it can be set all the time. You can be moving freely about the house, as can your pets, without fear of triggering a false alarm. The alarm can also be fully set at night. The only thing you cannot do, without turning off the alarm first, is to open any door or window, or to let roller blinds up with a thud. If the alarm is set with one or two upper windows open, however, they can remain so: only if you attempt to close them with the alarm on will the alarm be activated.

The disadvantages of the inertia system are cost and effectiveness in certain situations. If you have a lot of windows, this is not a cost-competitive system. You will find it almost certainly substantially cheaper to opt for a passive infra-red system (*see* p. 65). The problem of effectiveness concerns the type of window to be protected: if the window pane can be lifted out gently, without causing any vibration, the sensors will not be alerted. Leaded lights and sashes are particularly vulnerable. The system could, however, be backed up with metallic strips.

In conclusion, if your windows are of a type that could be effectively protected with this system and supplemented with magnetic door and window contacts, it is ideal in terms of convenience, particularly if you have pets and/or if you wish the entire house to be protected when you are in, particularly at night.

☐ Space detector systems

These are systems that measure the space in a room in terms of heat, sound or movement. If the characteristics of the room alter, as they would if someone walked into the room, the detectors signal this alteration to the control panel and the alarm is activated. The three systems that use this type of detection principle are passive infra-red, microwave and ultrasonic, of which the first is the most commonly used in domestic installations. The latter two rely essentially on the detection of movement, or the sound caused by movement, to and from the sensors. Both types of system emit continuous signals which hit all stable objects within their range and then bounce a certain proportion of the signal back to the detector. Each detector is in effect, therefore, a transceiver. When everything in the room is stable, the frequencies remain stable. The unit contains a comparitor which compares input with output. If someone enters the room, the frequency alters and the comparitor analyzes the speed of movement or sound frequency with the mass, to determine whether it is a person, rather than smaller changes in atmosphere due to humidity, air

Professional Systems

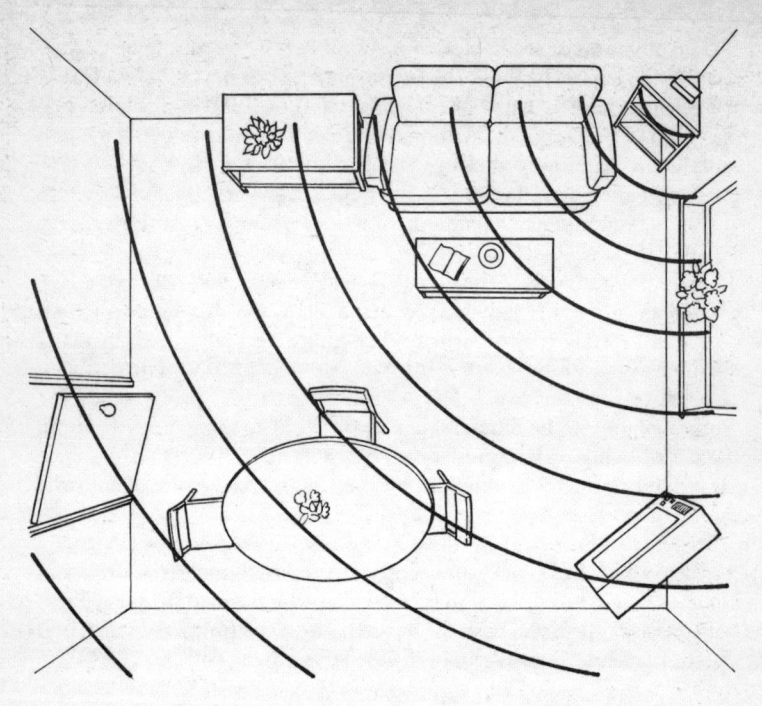

An ultrasonic system can detect any movement or heat increase in a room.

currents or a pet.

The differential between the incoming signals and the transmitted signals is known as the Doppler shift. The ultrasonic system transmits a signal between 25 and 50 kiloherz, whereas the microwave transmitter transmits at the much higher frequency of 10 gegaherz (million million herz). Whereas the ultrasonic system detects movement at distances of up to 12 m (40 ft), the microwave spans much greater distances.

Ultrasonic systems measure alterations in sound frequencies, while the microwave acts as a type of radar, detecting any pattern of movement in an environment that should be stable (in other words, devoid of things capable of movement, notably people and pets). Because ultrasonics respond to sound, there are some notable drawbacks to the system: a ringing telephone would activate the sensors, as would an answering machine giving out its message. A caged bird, such as a parrot or budgerigar, could presumably have the same effect. Once again, the electronic components of the system have to be

Professional Systems

professionally assessed and set. Because air itself carries ultrasonic sound – sound at a frequency beyond the range of human hearing – all the rooms protected must be free of draughts.

Microwave systems fare better in this respect, since they respond to actual movement rather than air turbulence; however, draughts can cause movement – of lampshades or curtains, for example – and the alarm will thus be activated. Pets have to be excluded from all the protected rooms of course. The only solution to this seems to be to keep pets out or to keep them in the kitchen and leave the kitchen unprotected on the grounds that there are fewer things worth stealing in that room than other rooms and that anything stolen from a kitchen can easily be replaced. Doors and windows can be protected with magnetic contacts, however, or with inertia sensors.

An additional disadvantage of the microwave system for the home user is the microwave's ability to penetrate glass (such as windows) and solid objects (like walls); this ability means that it can detect people beyond the area to be protected – even passing traffic. Installation of the system should be carried out only by an experienced professional, since mistakes are easily made in the initial setting. For example, if a microwave system is installed on a wet, rainy day, the moisture in the fabric of the house (ie bricks) absorbs energy and acts as a barrier to the microwave. Once this barrier is removed, on a dry and sunny day, the system's range will be increased and will therefore be able to detect movement at a greater distance, perhaps on the street outside your house.

Given the problems of ultrasonic and microwave systems for the domestic user, it is perhaps not surprising that passive infra-red systems are more commonly recommended. Of the space detection systems, they are apparently the least likely to give false alarms.

☐ Passive infra-red

Whereas ultrasonic systems measure sound and microwaves detect movement, passive infra-red devices measure heat. If someone walks into a room, the heat of their body is immediately picked up by the detector, relayed back to the comparitor, the differential assessed and the alarm activated. The advantages over the other volumetric systems are obvious: the alteration in the atmosphere must be caused by a living thing to give off heat, it may be assumed. Once again, pets have to be confined to a more or less unprotected kitchen.

There are, however, additional hazards inherent in the passive infra-red system. Heat given off by the sun and by central heating can cause the detectors to respond. If the detectors are so sited as to be affected by direct sunlight, false alarms may be generated. You may have left the house on a cloudy morning; by midday the sun may be blazing through the windows of your house. It is important, therefore, that the detectors are installed in such a position in each room that they cannot be affected by direct sunlight. Equally, while they will accept a gradual increase in temperature, such as that generated by central heating in the overall temperature of a room, they may trigger the alarm if they are sited directly above a powerful double radiator which is programmed to come on during the period of protection.

The major drawback of this, and all volumetric systems, is that they cannot be used to protect the house while you are in or if you wish your pets to be able to wander freely around the house. If you live in a house, rather than a flat, you will find that most professional systems allow you to set the alarm for one zone (downstairs), leaving the other zone (upstairs) unprotected, which is useful at night. This is satisfactory for some households but not all. The first drawback is that no one can go downstairs for a drink without turning off the alarm, and this is something that may be difficult to enforce if children live in the house. The second drawback is that some burglars are conversant with the various types of alarm systems. It is not uncommon for burglars to break into the upper storey of a house on the assumption that if the household are asleep, the upper storey must be unprotected.

Volumetric alarm systems must therefore be supplemented with effective window security (*see* Chapter 6), or with magnetic contacts or inertia sensors wired into the alarm system.

HOW TO CHOOSE

It is clearly the case that when an alarm company's surveyor makes his assessment of your needs, both you and he must take into account the following:

1 degree of risk of break-in

2 whether security is intended primarily for when you are out or for all the time

3 what supplements to the system are required in the way of physical deterrents (*see* Chapters 5, 6 and 7) and magnetic contacts or inertia sensors for doors and windows

4 cost.

You should also discuss the following:

1 location of alarm panel

How to Choose · Alarm Panel

2 location of external bell/siren
3 installation of panic buttons (*see* p.68)
4 is the alarm to be audible-only or connected to a central station?
5 number of keys supplied and keyholding arrangements
6 service and maintenance arrangements.

ALARM PANEL

The heart of the system, into which are wired all detectors and sensors, is contained within a small, neat box which has to be fixed to a wall in an inconspicuous spot. It needs to be reasonably near the main entrance so that you can get to it swiftly to turn off the alarm when you return home. It is usually located in a cupboard, often an understairs cupboard, near the front door. Burglars will know this, of course, so if your alarm company's surveyor can think of a location that is more unusual and yet still convenient, so much the better.

Alarm panels have an integral delay mechanism in order to give you time to reach them once you have opened the front door. These can be set for a certain number of seconds; 20–25 seconds is usually ideal. The period of delay should not be long because the alarm should be triggered as quickly as possible in the event of a break-in.

▶ *Alarm Bells*

The alarm panel should be located near a door so you can switch it off easily on entering.

EXTERNAL BELL

All alarm panels will have a delay mechanism, irrespective of whether they are audible-only units or connected to a central station. The external bell for an audible-only unit should be programmed to go off as quickly as possible. In practice, it will sound as soon as the delay mechanism period has expired, say, 20 seconds. It is designed to draw attention to neighbours and passers-by that your house is being burgled and to induce panic in the burglar in the hope of frightening him away.

If you elect for a system that when triggered alerts a central station silently, the function of the external bell is different. When the central station is alerted by a telephone automatic dialling mechanism, they should call the police who should attend; the external bell in this context serves to frighten away the burglar only in the event of any of the links of the system breaking down. For example, the telephone's automatic dialling mechanism may pick up a wrong number or a crossed line; the personnel at the central station may make an error of fact when they alert the police; the police may take so long to arrive, particularly in rural areas or in high risk city areas on a Friday evening, that the burglar is already a couple of miles away when they appear.

The question of the location of the external bell depends on the layout of your house. Ideally, it should be out of reach of windows, flat roofs, low walls and the ground, and in general as inaccessible as possible. The alarm panel should incorporate a feature that will cause the alarm to be activated if the external bell is tampered with. However, it should be borne in mind that some burglars have already developed a method of putting external bells out of action without causing the tamper feature to activate.

PANIC BUTTONS

These are a useful extra component of alarm systems in that they increase the householder's sense of peace of mind and provide additional security. They are referred to as personal attack buttons or PA buttons by alarm companies and are normally sited very near the front door and by one side of the bed in the master bedroom. They are connected into the alarm panel in such a way that they are active and ready for use whether or not the alarm system is actually switched on. So, if you happen to open your front door, having neglected to use the chain, limiter or spyhole, and find you are confronted with what looks like a suspicious caller or, worse still, with someone making a forcible entry, you simply press the PA button and this triggers the entire alarm system, external bell included, irrespective of whether the alarm is set. The point of having a PA button by your bedside is so that you can operate the alarm during the night; this is a useful back-up to those volumetric systems which by definition cannot be used to the full if you are in residence.

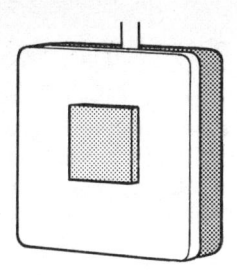

AUDIBLE-ONLY OR CENTRAL STATION CONNECTION

The determining factor in this decision, unfortunately, is very often cost. It is more expensive to have your alarm connected to the alarm company's headquarters and for them to guarantee the ncessary back-up in the event of a break-in. Apart from the obvious overheads, the chief factor contributing to the cost is the extraordinarily high number of false alarms. It is said to be as high as 98 per cent. It is for this reason that the police are now increasingly reluctant for an alarm to be connected directly to their emergency service. You have instead to choose a security company of sufficient size (not the local electrician, in other words) to guarantee constant monitoring on a 24-hour basis and the appropriate back-up.

Central station linking is recommended if you can afford it, or if the situation is so high risk that you have no choice.

NUMBER OF KEYS

Alarm companies never supply enough. Make sure that you ask them for a key for each regular member of the household and two extras (one for a regular visitor such as a nanny or daily help and the other to be used when you have guests to stay). All the experts will urge you to have as few keys as possible and never to lend them; in practice, however, this is not realistic if you are at work all day.

KEYHOLDING

If you are out at work all day and if you are away, you must inform the police that you have had an alarm installed and let them know who holds the keys in the event of an attempted break-in or a false alarm. Keys can be lodged with a friendly neighbour for safe keeping, or possibly a local shop. If you have already asked a neighbour to keep an eye on your house while you are away (*see* Chapter 4), it is clearly more practical for her to have them.

SERVICE AND MAINTENANCE

If your alarm is connected to a central station, a service and maintenance agreement is recommended, if not *de rigueur*. If it is audible-only, a maintenance agreement is still recommended; make sure that it covers not only an annual service but an unlimited number of free call-outs for false alarms. At current rates, this is most unlikely to be less than £80 plus VAT.

USING IT

A burglar alarm only works if it is used. That may seem obvious, but an extraordinarily large number of people feel so well protected by simply having the alarm that they tend not to use it for short trips out or at night. Given that most burglaries are committed during the day and can be accomplished in under half an hour, it is rash not to put it on even if you are only popping next door. Two minutes can easily turn into twenty and the loss of many treasured possessions and a great deal of disruption. So, if you have decided that your security and peace of mind is worth investing several hundred pounds in a burglar alarm, do make use of your investment.

·9·

EXTERNAL FORCES

If you live in a house rather than a flat, particularly out of a city or town, you should give some thought to what is known as perimeter protection. This in essence means securing your boundaries and gates. To what degree you are prepared to take this security depends partly upon what kind of area you live in and partly what value you place upon the things in your house and outbuildings. Some forms of perimeter protection described in this chapter are designed to be used either in very high risk areas or by wealthy people with the resources and motivation to make a considerable investment. Even if this does not apply to you, there are a number of ways in which you can improve your security simply, cheaply and effectively.

ENTRYPHONE

This could be regarded as an extension of door security, which is the subject of Chapter 5, but it may also be regarded as a form of perimeter protection in that the unit may be placed not only at the front door, or

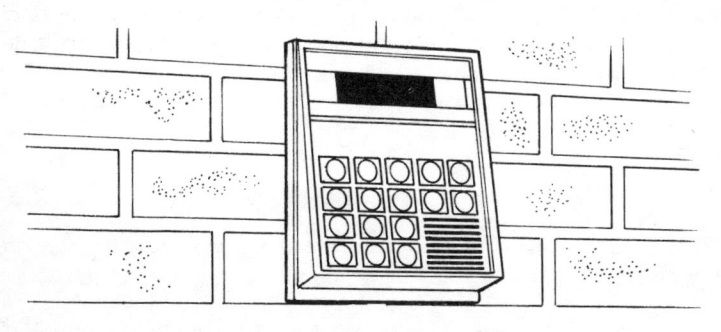

Entryphones are becoming more and more common security precautions.

main door to a block of flats, but by your gate down the drive. Chubb market a number of units designed both for the consumer and for military and defence uses. Some incorporate video units so that you may take a look at your caller, without them knowing, before you decide whether or not to admit. This type of device is particularly useful if you are normally some distance away from the front door, or wherever it is sited, and want to be sure that your caller is genuine, without wasting your time and energy.

PORCHES

Well-secured glazed porches are considered to be a good deterrent to burglars and this is because the burglar has first to break into the porch and, in sight of passers-by, he has in addition to force the front door. If you have a porch, make sure that the glass is tough, resistant to attack and securely fitted into its frames. Old crumbling putty provides a burglar with an opportunity for lifting out an entire sheet noiselessly.

Because porches are a good deterrent to burglars, you should consider the fact that this in turn focuses a burglar's attention on your back or side door, French windows, or any easily accessible windows. Burglars are quick to seize upon any weak spot, so your guiding principle should always be to make your entire home as *uniformly* secure as you can afford.

GATES

This is where you have to assess your own situation and weigh the degree of risk against the investment involved. It is possible, of course, to have 3.6 m (12 ft) high wrought iron gates, topped with fearsome spikes, monitored with videoscan and operated by remote electronic control. Most home owners would regard this as an excessive level of security, but not so those with a few million pounds' worth of priceless pictures and family jewelry.

BOUNDARIES

This level of security must be consistent to be effective. This means all boundaries have to be made impenetrable – and of course the gates must be closed and locked every time you leave and return to the house. Boundaries can be made impenetrable and insurmountable if the degree of risk justifies the investment. 3.6 m (12 ft) high walls can be topped with vicious shards of glass sunk into the concrete or with electrified wire. Electrified fences are also a possibility in high risk situations. As with downpipe security, you must install a warning notice if boundary protection of this kind is used to avoid possible prosecution under either the Householders' Liabilities Act or the Highways Act.

Walls are easier than hedges or fencing to make intruder proof and should be regarded as the only option in any high risk situation; an exception to this would be electrified wire fencing such as you might see around prisons and alongside the Berlin Wall. Ordinary wooden fencing could be fitted with electrified wire, but it would still be vulnerable.

Hedges can be made to look less inviting to an intruder by planting with holly and hawthorn, but both these take some years to become established. A professional burglar would regard a dense hedge as more of a nuisance than a deterrent.

If you live in a very high risk situation, apart from electrified boundaries you should also consider installing closed circuit TV or videoscan equipment. Clearly, this requires some considerable investment, not just for the equipment, but also for the back-up required. For this type of monitoring you need staff to watch the screens, or automatic devices to signal to a central station that an intruder has triggered the alarm. There is no doubt that these systems have their drawbacks in that they can be triggered by animals – and yet every alarm must be fully investigated.

An alternative would be to fit microwave or laser beams to cover the area around your house in the same way that a burglar alarm does inside the house. As soon as the beam picks up the presence of an intruder, it is triggered. Clearly, with this sort of protection, you must have some sort of electronically operated system on the gates which you can control from the house; otherwise every time the postman comes he will trigger the alarm.

Another alternative is to fit microphones to external boundaries so that they are in effect wired for sound: as soon as an intruder attempts to negotiate walls or fencing, the alarm is activated, irrespective of how little noise he may make. The sound generated by the movement of clothes is sufficient to activate this type of alarm. However, this type of alarm can also be besieged by false alarms generated by animals.

MAKING USE OF LIGHTING

The majority of burglaries are committed during the day when the householder is most likely to be out. However, it is essential to have good night time security as well and, if you base this on the use of lighting, it need not be that expensive. Not only is it comparatively simple to install, it is also modestly priced, effective and offers an added bonus of convenience for members of the household. Again, a cheaper option is to plug several table lamps into electrical time switches to give the impression that people are at home.

If your street is not well lit, or if your house is set back from the road, give some thought to having automatic lights installed. These can be put in anywhere around the house: by the entrance gate, by the garage, at the four points of the exterior of the house and fixed to the house looking down or across the garden. The lights are fixed with the switch permanently in the ON position; they come on, however, only when someone walks across their zone of detection. They are, of course, subject to 'false alarms' in that they can be triggered by dogs, cats, foxes and birds; but they should suffice to deter an opprotunist burglar in a poorly lit, not too high risk, situation. They are also very convenient for you when you return home in the dark and indeed provide an element

Making Use of Lighting

An automatic light outside your front door will deter burglars and ease your entry to the house.

of personal protection at night. Once the lights have been activated, they will stay on for a period that has been pre-set (anything from 5–20 minutes) and then automatically switch off. If you have cats or other animals around, particularly nocturnal animals such as badgers and foxes, you will find the system demands a fairly frequent replacement of light bulbs, especially during the winter with increased hours of darkness. But the system as a whole does not need to be expensive to run as the unit can be solar powered. The unit can be wired into your existing outside lights or wired into bright spotlights.

▶ *External Forces*

PROVIDING COVER

One of the things that you can easily eliminate from your property is good cover for a potential burglar. The more open the approach to the house, the better. If your house is secluded with shrubs and trees growing all around it, however attractive that may look, the situation is ideal for a burglar either during the day or at night. The ideal setting for a country house is one in which it can be approached only by a long, straight and open drive, clearly visible from the road.

A FAST GETAWAY

Police and security experts are agreed that the majority of burglaries in country and rural areas take place in those houses situated near motorways or 'A' roads. A burglar likes to feel he can make a fast getaway and merge into the rest of the traffic as soon as possible. He will not be attracted to a property a couple of miles up an unmade road, unless he knows the pickings will be very rich and he has an accomplice as a lookout – or perhaps he has even arranged in advance for the householder to be out. When you are house-hunting, therefore, think of the situation of the house in the context of security; discuss the area in general, too, with the local police who usually prove helpful with this type of enquiry.

THE GARAGE AND OUTBUILDINGS

There is no need here for high level security, simply because it is possible to make outbuildings firmly secure for a modest outlay.

Garages and outbuildings represent a treasure trove to a burglar who may find not only cars, motorbikes, cycles, scooters, golf clubs and gardening equipment, but also all the tools he needs, including a ladder, to break into your house. In country areas, the garage is often the burglar's first stop, and it is essential that it has a good security lock. As an alternative, fit a good quality closed shackle padlock, such as a Chubb, available from your local locksmith. Windows should be fitted with window locks and bars if they are more than 13 cm (5 in) in depth. Any ladders should be independently fitted with their own closed shackle padlock, regardless of the fact that they are put away in a locked garage.

All the equipment that is commonly found in garages, from cars to cycles to lawnmowers can be engraved with your postcode as described in Chapter 2. In the event that they are stolen and subsequently

The Garage and Outbuildings

recovered, you will at least be able to make a positive identification. This should be regarded as last resort security, however; your aim should be to prevent a burglar even getting in to the garage or any outbuildings that house equipment with a good re-sale value.

If you wish to take the security of your garage and its contents one step further, consider having electronically operated garage doors fitted, for which you use a remote control device. You will find the companies that supply and fit these in Yellow Pages under the headings of Doors, Up and Over and/or Garage Equipment.

The added advantage of electronically operated garage doors, beyond their value as a security device, is that of convenience for the household. You can simply drive straight in or straight out without having to get out of the car.

Do remember that an open garage, devoid of a car, is a golden invitation to a burglar: it says simply, 'We're out, help yourself and there's the ladder and all the tools you need'.

If you have gates, these too can be fitted with electronic remote controlled devices so that, again, you need not get out of the car to open/close them. (If you do not have such a device fitted, be sure to spare a few seconds – even in the rain or snow – to get out and close the gates as you leave.)

▶ External Forces

GOING OUT

Before you leave the house always make a quick security check that you have not left any obvious sign that there is no one at home, and make the most of your security devices:

1 put on the Ansaphone (see Chapter 2)
2 check all window locks and back and side doors
3 make sure that you have brought in any deliveries, such as post, milk, newspapers
4 put on the burglar alarm and lock the front door
5 take a good look round to make sure that there is nothing unusual left out.
6 close and lock garage doors and gates before you leave

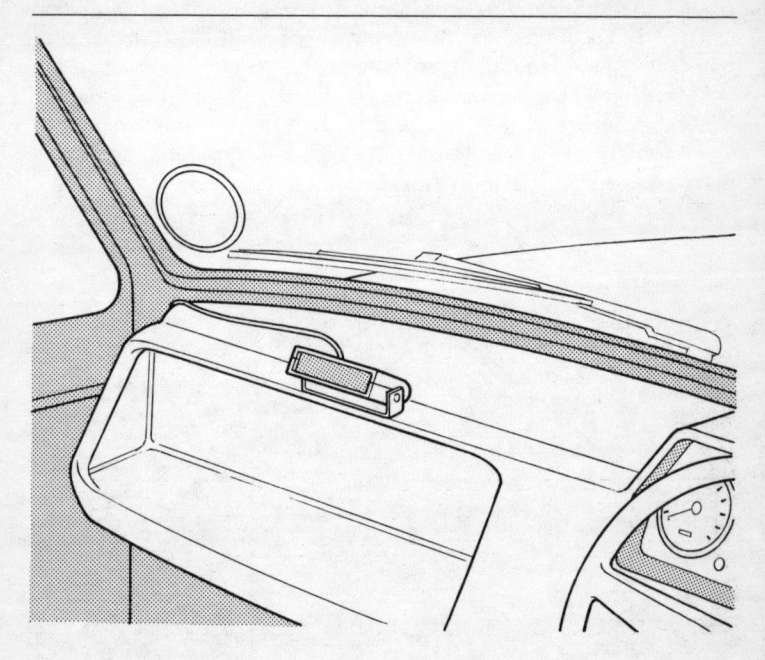

A car alarm can be easily installed on most car dashboards.

CAR SECURITY

Car theft is becoming increasingly common, with many cars being stolen from outside their owner's house. Cars are also stolen from car

Car Security

parks of all sorts (below and above ground), side streets, outside pubs, village shopping streets – in short, it makes little difference where you park a car, but it does matter how you secure it.

A *Which?* report in 1986 noted that security on virtually every make of car was 'inadequate'. First of all, although you should always close the windows and lock all the doors and the boot whenever you leave your car, you should not rely on the locks for security. It is easy to obtain duplicates and it is also easy to pick most car locks. Smashing a window is not difficult, either, although it is noisy and may attract unwelcome attention.

No car can be said to be properly secured until it is fitted with a good car alarm that is operated by a concealed switch, or operated by pushing a certain spot on the dashboard with a magnet, the location of the spot being known only to the car owner. Most other types of car

▶ *External Forces*

· 79 ·

alarm are known to thieves and they are familiar with ways of dismantling them. Engineers in Sweden are currently experimenting with car alarms that give an electric shock to the unsuspecting thief. It may well be only a matter of years before this idea is put into production.

Car theft is already very common, but theft from cars is even more so. People living and working in our big cities have sometimes had not one, not two but three successive car radios or stereos stolen from their car. To prevent this, fitting an alarm is recommended and so is investing in a removable radio/cassette. You take it with you when you lock and leave the car. Do not be tempted to put it in the glove compartment of the boot: car thieves know perfectly well that this is what many people do. You can also avoid drawing attention to the fact that you have a car radio by having an automatically retractable aerial fitted: as you switch off the radio, the aerial automatically retracts.

Never, ever leave anything in the car or on the seats – not even if you are just visiting someone for a quick cup of tea. Always keep the car completely empty and store any shopping or your briefcase in the boot.

YOUR OWN SECURITY

All the measures described in this and previous chapters are designed for the protection of your home and your possessions and are intended to encourage your awareness for the need for better security at a time when the crime rate is increasing significantly each year.

Your personal security, however, should be regarded as even more important than that of your possessions. Such measures as using spyholes before opening the front door and only then opening it on a chain; locking doors and windows at night; and having good lighting around the house, all contribute to your personal safety at home.

Women are more likely than men to be attacked, and, particularly if you are a woman, you should bear these recommendations in mind when you are out:

1 Do not sit alone in a individual railway carriage if it is empty or if there is one male occupant.

2 Try to avoid deserted areas at night.

3 Do not use underground railway systems late at night if it means having to walk through long, deserted subways.

4 If you are a woman motorist, do not allow yourself to be flagged down at night.

5 Do not walk through alleys either at day or night.

Your Own Security

6 If ever you suspect that you are being followed, ring the bell of the first front door you see and ask for assistance.

7 Always try to keep to well-lit areas at night. Walk on the road rather than dimly lit pavements or paths.

8 If you live in a high risk, inner city area, carry a personal screech alarm with you at all times.

9 As you reach home, have your keys handy so that you can let yourself in without delay. Lock the front door and put the chain in place.

·10·

'HOW DID THEY GET IN?'

If you have read the previous chapters and put into practice the recommendations for securing your home against burglary, you should not have to address yourself to the question 'How did they get in?' Unfortunately, however, many of us tend to think about home security after a burglary rather than before. This is still worth it, of course, not least because burglars are aware that most people replace their losses with their insurance within two to three months – and the burglar then frequently strikes again.

FINDING A BURGLAR IN YOUR HOME

If, as you return home, you find anything amiss, such as the front door open, or chained, someone moving around inside, or a window thrown open, do not under any circumstances make an attempt to enter the house. Simply go to a neighbour's and dial 999 for the police. Once you have done this, see if you can spot any unfamiliar car in the road: take a note of its make, colour and registration number.

If you enter the house and only then discover that there is an intruder, leave as quickly as possible and, as above, dial 999 for the police. If you are unlucky enough to come face to face with an intruder, run: do not attempt to detain him. Not only is he likely to be stronger than you, but he will also be in a state of panic and therefore likely to lash out indiscriminately.

A night time intruder is perhaps the most frightening of possibilities. If, for some reason, he has not triggered your alarm, do so yourself with the panic button at the side of the bed (*see* Chapter 8). If you do not have an alarm incorporating such a device, the police recommend that you keep absolutely still and pretend to be asleep on the grounds that a burglar seeks to steal possessions rather than harm people. If frightened, however, the burglar may well harm you in his desire not to be caught and not to be recognized at a later date. Although getting up

Finding a Burglar · Discovering a Burglary

and investigating, and putting all the lights on, is a natural reaction, it is not recommended.

DISCOVERING A BURGLARY

The majority of burglaries take place when the house is empty, so it is much more likely that you will return home to find that you have been burgled and the burglar has left.

1 Do not touch anything.

2 Do not tidy up, although you will obviously be keen to do so.

3 Once you are certain that the burglar has left, call the police.

4 Resist the temptation to tidy up. Instead, make a cup of tea or have a drink. Then, while you await the police, make a list of anything odd that you notice and any visible sign of forced entry.

5 Make a list of things that you can see have been stolen. Add, as queries, those items that could have been stolen and which you will have to check later when you are allowed to touch things.

6 When the police arrive, let them look over the entire house even if the burglary was confined to one room. Make sure that they take fingerprints. In inner city areas, where there are so many burglaries, they may feel it is not worth it; make sure that they do so, nevertheless, unless they give a convincing reason why they should not do so. These can be put to the police bank of fingerprints; it may be that the burglary has been committed by a criminal already known to them.

7 Ask the police as they leave to arrange to have the Crime Prevention Officer call on you.

▶ *How Did They Get In?*

REPAIRING THE DAMAGE

Once the police have left, your first step must be to call your locksmith to check your locks, repair any damaged ones and, if the burglar has stolen a set of your keys, to replace all locks.

You can obtain a reputable locksmith by asking the local police or by personal recommendation. Alternatively, you may ask their professional association (*see* Useful Names and Addresses) to recommend one in your area; or you may choose to use a security company.

Repairing the Damage · Reducing Your Losses

The next step is to call a glazier to replace any damaged glass. Remember that when a window is replaced, the putty remains soft for a day or two; burglars sometimes smash a window, which makes a lot of noise, prior to committing a burglary. Once they have observed the window has been replaced, they return and remove the new pane soundlessly from the frame, while the putty is still soft, in order to break in with the minimum trouble and minimum noise.

You may also need a builder if a door frame has been smashed or damaged. The cost of repairs to doors, windows and locks can all be recovered from the Buildings section of your insurance policy, so remember to ask for and keep receipts for all such jobs. The quicker the repair work can be done, the better in that it will help you psychologically to recover from the intrusion, at the same time ensuring that it is more difficult for the burglar to pay a return visit.

REDUCING YOUR LOSSES

The next step is to inform your bank and other financial organizations of any cheque books, pass books or credit cards that may have been stolen. Check the following:

- cheque book
- chequecard
- joint account cheque book and its chequecards
- Servicetill card
- Eurocheques and Eurochequecard
- travellers' cheques
- building society passbook
- post office book
- pension book
- American Express card
- Diner's Club card
- Access card
- Barclaycard
- store cards, such as Marks & Spencer, Harrods, John Lewis, for example

You should telephone each organization, giving them your name, address and number of the card, together with the date of its theft. You should follow this with a written confirmation of those facts; this is in order to protect yourself at a later date when it may be discovered that the burglar has sold on some of your cards and your accounts are showing mystifying debits. Your liability for these debits usually ends from the time that you have reported the loss of the card or chequebook.

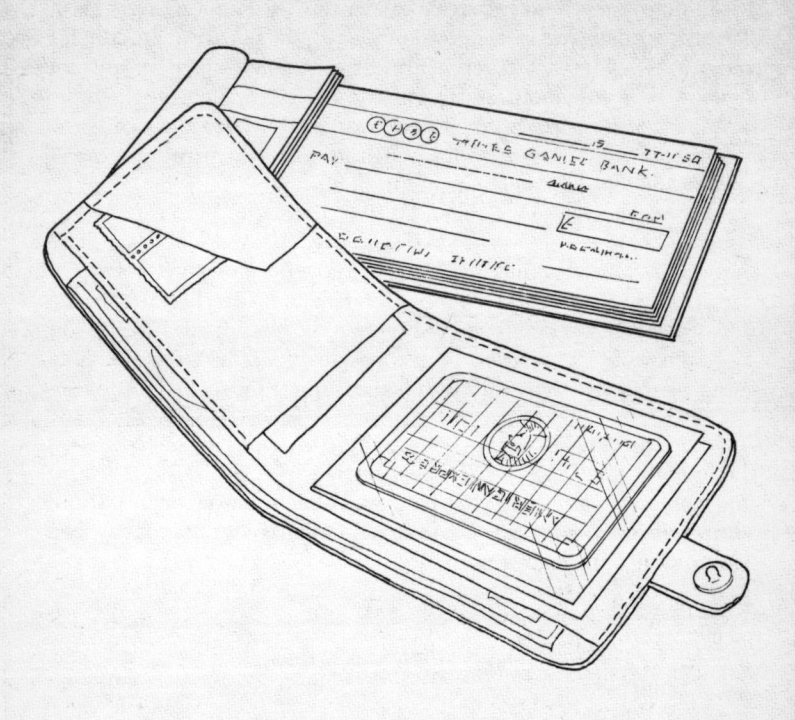

PASSPORT

Check that your passport has not been stolen. These have a substantial resale value once in the hands of certain criminals. Report the loss at once to the Passport Office, Petty France, London SW1. If you are intending to travel shortly, ask them how long it will take to obtain a replacement; if necessary, arrange for alternative documentation, available from the Post Office.

CARDS AND TICKETS

The next step in what seems an interminable process in the aftermath of a burglary, is to check your collection tickets, your membership

cards and tickets for any performances.
Check the following:

- drycleaning tickets
- shoe repair tickets
- jewelry repair tickets
- library tickets
- membership cards of clubs and professional associations tickets for theatre, opera, circus etc

I suspect that it is unlikely that a burglar would make use of any of these, but the aim is for you to be able to reclaim whatever you would otherwise lose as a result of the tickets being missing.

INSURANCE

Provided that you informed the police straightaway, or within 24 hours of the discovery of the burglary at the most, you can safely leave informing your insurance company until after you have done all the things described above. You should ask your insurance company for a claim form in respect of possessions, known as Contents or Personal Effects, and, if necessary, an additional form for damage to your home, covered under Buildings.

If you do not receive the form within one week, remind your insurance company that you are still awaiting the form.

When you receive the form, give all the details as requested, which may include the date of purchase, the supplier, the model number, the amount of depreciation, together with supporting documentation. This can take the form of receipts, guarantee cards, credit card vouchers if fully filled in, photographs, jeweller's valuations.

When you return the completed claim form to your insurers, make sure that you note in a covering letter that the form covers all the items so far known to be missing. It is common for the victim of a burglary to realize only weeks, sometimes months later, that there is something they have overlooked.

Make sure that you photostat the complete form, together with all the supporting documentation in case of loss in the post.

PROCESSING YOUR CLAIM

When your insurers receive your completed form, they will verify the details with the suppliers listed, verify the event of the burglary itself with the police, and conduct any further enquiries that they judge to be necessary in establishing that the claim is a genuine one.

If the claim is for more than a certain amount, the insurers will appoint a loss adjuster or loss assessor to visit you and discuss the claim with you. The amount varies according to which company it is: it can be £200 or it may be as much as £500. If the insurers should feel an investigation is demanded, this will also cause them to despatch a loss adjuster to your home.

It is known that the victims of burglaries sometimes tend to exaggerate the value of the items that they have lost as a means of compensating themselves for the trauma and inconvenience they have suffered. Because of this, loss adjusters tend to interrogate closely all claimants. Even if they receive satisfactory answers during this interrogation, they may still make you an offer in full and final settlement of the claim. It hardly needs saying that the offer frequently falls short of the amount claimed.

Do not allow yourself to be harassed in this way. Provided that you have made a completely fair and honest claim, you have every right to stand firm and to be compensated with the full amount claimed. If the loss adjuster raises the issue of depreciation and deterioration of certain items, consult your policy: if it states that your possessions are covered for full replacement value, any depreciation is irrelevant. You should also bear in mind that while electrical appliances deteriorate, real jewelry does not. In fact, it appreciates in value and this is something that you should bear in mind when renewing your policy each year.

When the claim is finally processed, you will probably be sent a form to sign that states you accept their cheque 'in full and final settlement' of the claim. You should alter this, making it clear that you accept their cheque in settlement of the claim as submitted and that you reserve your right to make a further claim if it transpires that additional items, which you had not noticed at the time, have been stolen.

Once the claim is settled, consult your insurers about amending your policy. If all your jewelry has been stolen, for example, you need no longer have it covered under the insurance. If you intend to replace everything that was stolen virtually straightaway, there is no need to amend the policy; but have a word with your insurers in any case.

A REPEAT PERFORMANCE?

Burglars are known to return to the scene of successful burglaries a few months later on the assumption that the householder will by then have replaced the valuables that the burglar stole in the first instance. In order to prevent this happening, you should scrutinize your home for

A Repeat Performance?

its level of security.

Firstly, contact the Crime Prevention Officer at your local police station and ask him to visit your home in order to assess its security. Listen to his recommendations and discuss any points that you are uncertain about. If you decide to use any professionals, such as locksmiths or burglar alarm installers, ask the Crime Prevention Officer to let you have a list of companies in your area.

If you intend to have security work carried out, be sure to obtain at least three estimates from each type of company in accordance with the recommendations given in previous chapters.

Finally, after you have been burgled beware of over-reacting to the extent of buying a dog. A dog is an effective deterrent only while it is there – and not necessarily then. When you take it out for a walk, your home will be as vulnerable as it was before. Furthermore, puppies are not much of a deterrent: a good security dog needs to be fully grown and professionally trained.

APPENDIX

USEFUL ORGANIZATIONS & ADDRESSES

E Aldridge & Son Ltd
50 Queen Street
Salford
Manchester M3 7DQ
Tel: 061-834 1676
locks, safes, anti-climb paint

Also at:
Silca House
30–34 Eagle Wharf Road
London N1 7EB
Tel: 01-251 4791
fluorescent markers

Banham Locks & Alarms Ltd
233–235 Kensington High Street
London W8 6SF
Tel: 01-937 4311
locks, safes, alarm systems

Berol Ltd
Oldmeadow Road
King's Lynn
Norfolk PE20 4JR
Tel: 0553-761221
marker pens

British Security Industry Association
68 St James's Street
London SW1A 1PH
Tel: 01-439 6634
trade association

Camrex Ltd
Camrex House
P.O. Box 34
Washington
Tyne & Wear NE37 1QJ
Tel: 091-417000
anti-climb paint

INDEX

absence 4, 6, 9–11, 29–32, 39, 78
Ansaphone messages 9, 11, 29–30

bogus callers 50–3
boundary security 72–4
burglar alarms 6–7, 54, 70
 advantages 56-7, 66–7
 alarm panel 67
 car 79–80
 central station linking 69
 external bell 68
 magnetic contacts 59, 60
 panic buttons 68–9
 pressure mats 59–60
 professional systems 61–6
 service and maintenance 70
 supply and fitting 57–8
 types 58–9
burglary
 discovering 82–3
 during occupation 14
 fast getaway routes 76
 methods of entry 5, 33, 37, 40, 47
 opportunist 6, 10, 56–7
 prevalence 4, 5
 professionally planned 10

car security 7, 78–80
cellar security 49–50
closed circuit television 73–4

dogs, as deterrents 14, 36, 61, 89
do-it-yourself
 alarm systems 59–61
 as fire hazard 22
door chains and limiters 35
door hinges 35
door keys 39
doors
 back 36–8
 front 33–6
 garage 77
 patio 38
door viewers 35

electrical equipment
 as fire hazard 15–16, 21, 23, 24
engraving, personal items 12
entryphones 35–6, 71–2

fencing 73
fire drill 25
fire escape routes 25, 27
fire extinguishers 16, 28
firefighting 27–8
fire hazards 15, 16, 20, 21, 23, 24, 27–8, 36
fire precautions 7, 15–16, 23
 see also smoke detectors
fire prevention 4
 and children 22
 and DIY 22
 and housework 20–1
 at night 24
 in the kitchen 23

Index

in the living room 23

garage security 7, 50, 76–7
gates 72, 77
glass
   laminated 41
   patio door 38
   replacing 85
   wire reinforced 41
glass structures security 50

heat detectors 17

illegal entry 5, 33, 37, 40, 47
   damage 84–5
   see also burglary
insurance
   claims 87–8
   for burglary damage repair work 84–5

key security 39, 44–5, 69, 70

letter-box security 33
lights, automatic 30–1, 74–5
locking devices 33
   bolts 36
   closed shackle padlock 76
   five lever security mortise deadlock 35
   key access 36
   mortise security bolts 37–8
   ten lever locks 35
   window 41–5

Marked Property stickers 13
marking, possessions 11–13
microphones 74
microwaves 9

Neighbourhood Watch 13
noise, as a deterrent 14

paint, anti-climb 49
passport theft 86
personal attack buttons 68–9
personal belongings 8, 9, 11–14, 30, 85–7
personal security 80–2
physical deterrents 6, 14, 16, 55–6
police 4, 5, 6–7, 68, 69, 83, 87
porches, as a deterrent 72
postcode marking 13

roof hatches 47–8

screech alarms 81
security marker pens 11
security precautions 4, 29–30, 78
   assessment 88–9
   levels of 6–7, 55
   vigilance 45
skylight security 49
smoke detectors
   false alarm triggers 18–19
   ionization 17
   location 19, 20
   methods of power 17–18
   optical 17
   supply and fitting 19
stolen property 5, 85–7

vandalism, during burglary 9
video scan units 72, 74

walls 72–3
windows 40–1
   casement 44
   cellar 49–50
   locks 41
   louvre 41
   sash 42–3
   telescopic gates and grills 41, 50